WITHIN ARM'S LENGTH

WITHIN ARM'S LENGTH

THE EXTRAORDINARY LIFE AND CAREER OF A SPECIAL AGENT

IN

THE UNITED STATES SECRET SERVICE

DAN EMMETT

Special Agent,
United States Secret Service (Retired)

iUniverse, Inc.
Bloomington

Within Arm's Length
The Extraordinary Life and Career of a Special
Agent in the United States Secret Service

iUniverse books may be ordered through booksellers or by contacting:

iUniverse
1663 Liberty Drive
Bloomington, IN 47403
www.iuniverse.com
1-800-Authors (1-800-288-4677)

ISBN: 978-1-4620-7072-5 (sc)
ISBN: 978-1-4620-7073-2 (hc)
ISBN: 978-1-4620-7074-9 (e)

Library of Congress Control Number: 2011961646

Printed in the United States of America

iUniverse rev. date: 01/11/2012

For the men and women of the United States Secret Service who have made the ultimate sacrifice in the service of our nation.

Contents

PREFACE

In the Home of President John F. Kennedy, November 1984

From May 16, 1983, until May 16, 2004, I served as a special agent in the United States Secret Service. There I was afforded both the honor and tremendous responsibility of protecting three sitting presidents of the United States.

During the span of that career, I learned above all else that there is no such thing as a routine day in the Secret Service. Anything was possible, from the boredom of answering telephones in the office to flying on board Air Force One or perhaps going for a morning run with the president of the United States.

Such was the case on a late November day in 1984 when, one year out of agent school, I found myself temporarily assigned to protect Senator Ted Kennedy at the Kennedy family compound in Hyannis Port, Massachusetts.

The main compound included the home formerly owned by the patriarch of the family, Ambassador Joseph P. Kennedy, along with another house across the driveway that had been owned by the late Robert F. Kennedy. By 1984, ownership of the ambassador's home had been relinquished to Senator Kennedy, and Bobby Kennedy's home was owned by his widow, Ethel.

Nearby sat another house, which faced one of three streets bordering the compound. The house at 111 Irving Avenue was a large Cape Cod, with gray shingle siding, and had once been owned by the late President John F. Kennedy.

I had seen the house every day since arriving at Hyannis Port and was aware it had once belonged to President Kennedy but knew little more about it. I had assumed it was simply an empty or nearly empty house that was at one time the summer home of the thirty-fifth president of the United States.

On the thirtieth and final day of our assignment, Senator Kennedy hosted a party in appreciation for his Secret Service agents, who for the past month had been willing to trade their lives for his if necessary. Late in the afternoon, as the festivities began to dwindle and almost everyone had departed for the airport and home, Kennedy moved among the few agents who remained and asked if anyone would like to tour his brother's house, meaning the home of the late President John F. Kennedy. Intrigued by the prospect of walking through President Kennedy's home, I accepted the senator's offer, as did two other agents.

After obtaining keys to the home from the estate's caretaker, who greatly resembled Spencer Tracy from *The Old Man and the Sea*, the senator escorted us three agents on the short walk to the back entrance of President Kennedy's house. After unlocking the door and allowing us entry, the senator handed me the key and said, "Here, Dan, please lock it up when you are done." He then turned and walked back to the main house, leaving behind members of the latest generation of Secret Service agents assigned to protect a Kennedy with total access to the home of the late president.

It took only moments after entering the house for me to realize it had not received the news of President Kennedy's death. Frozen in time, it seemed to be waiting for its windows to again vibrate, announcing the arrival of a helicopter delivering the president and his family for another weekend or holiday at Hyannis Port with friends and a multitude of relatives. It had now been waiting in silence for twenty-one years.

At first glance, the president's home seemed much like any other and was furnished as expected, with furniture and décor that ranged from antique through early 1960s, complemented by an abundant supply of *Life* magazines and newspapers. The subtle clue that this home was perhaps not like others began with the discovery that these reading materials were all printed in 1963 or earlier.

As the other two agents and I began to explore the old house, laced with a hint of dampness from the late New England autumn, my colleagues each took a quick look around and then declared they had to leave for the airport or miss their flights. As I bade farewell to my comrades, I realized I should have probably gone with them, but I was not yet ready to end this once-in-a-lifetime opportunity.

Now alone, I moved through the house and slowly began to discover a museum's worth of President Kennedy's personal belongings. As I allowed this more-than-unique experience to sink in, a revelation occurred: I was walking through a time capsule, an inner sanctum that probably few outside the Kennedy family had seen since 1963.

Some of the priceless items that now surrounded me included framed photographs of President Kennedy and his family, both on the walls and resting on various tables and shelves. Other items I stood before included business suits in President Kennedy's closet, which upon closer examination revealed his name sewn inside by someone possessing great skill in such matters. Arranged neatly on wooden hangers, each seemed to be waiting for President Kennedy to return and wear it once again.

While continuing to explore, a feeling of uneasiness began to set in, making me feel I had inadvertently surpassed the boundaries Senator Kennedy had intended when offering access to the home. It was time to leave.

As I prepared to depart the bedroom and the house that time had forgotten, two items lying on President Kennedy's dresser suddenly caught my attention. Curious, I moved closer for a more detailed examination—and found a pair of gold cuff links. Standing in the cold bedroom of the late president, surrounded by the fading light of Election Day 1984, I read the initials engraved on the face of each accessory and realized to whom they had once belonged. There really was no such thing as a routine day in the Secret Service.

ACKNOWLEDGMENTS

Thanks go to the following persons, without whom this book would never have been completed.

For my wife, also a retired agent, whose invaluable assistance kept me on the right path throughout this process.

For my son, who patiently seemed to understand why I was not always available to spend more time with him as I sat in my office writing for hours and days on end.

For my mother and father, who provided me with an education and the values that have sustained me throughout life.

And total gratitude, more than mere thanks, to the United States Marine Corps, for its invaluable assistance in helping transform me from a boy into a man.

CHAPTER 1

The Death of a President
and Birth of a Career

Through the years, many people have asked how and why I chose the Secret Service as a career. The answer lies somewhere in the inescapable fact that children are highly impressionable.

On November 22, 1963, an event occurred that made such an indelible mark on my young life, it largely determined who and what I was to become as an adult. That event was the assassination of President John F. Kennedy, and I was eight years old at the time.

Over the course of that fateful weekend as an idealistic third grader, I made the decision that one of my career goals in life was to become a Secret Service agent, one of the men who protected the president of the United States. Two decades later, that was precisely what I did. This is the story of that career, first imagined as a child, that through hard work and a bit of good fortune flourished into reality.

Beginnings

The third of three sons, I was born in 1955 at the end of the baby boom in the small town of Gainesville, Georgia, located about fifty miles northeast of Atlanta. Each of my brothers and I were born six years apart, so that none were in college at the same time. That is how carefully my parents planned things.

Dad in an unusually relaxed pose during a family vacation circa 1957

(Personal collection of Dan Emmett)

While neither of my parents had progressed in formal education beyond the high school level, both were determined that my two brothers and I would all graduate from college. Through great sacrifices characteristic of their generation, we all did.

My father and mother were born in 1919 and 1920, respectively, and were products of the Great Depression. Both had grown up in families with little money, but through hard work and good financial planning, they accomplished amazing things together in their fifty-nine years of marriage. That partnership ended only after Dad passed away in 1999.

My father was a very serious, totally self-made man, who, without warning, could display a very colorful sense of humor that at times caused my mother to recoil in horror. Partial to dark suits with white shirts and dark, thin ties, he greatly resembled former Secretary of Defense Robert McNamara, complete with wire-rimmed glasses and swept-back dark hair. A World War II veteran of the Pacific Theater of Operations, he was extremely patriotic and was an active member of both the American Legion and the Veterans of Foreign Wars. The son of a Baptist minister, Dad loved God first, his family second, and baseball third, although the order could vary at times depending on what teams were in the World Series.

After marrying my mother in 1940, Dad discovered, mostly as the result of her promptings, that he possessed a talent for business and escaped his dead-end life of working in a cotton mill by becoming a furniture salesman. In 1950, Dad started his own furniture business, appropriately named Emmett Furniture, which he owned for over sixteen years and then sold for a decent profit.

My mother was the quintessential mom of the late 1950s and early 1960s. Always perfectly attired and resembling a TV mom, she vacuumed and cleaned our immaculate home in dresses and pearls. In spite of her hectic schedule, she always had dinner on the table each evening promptly at six o'clock when my father arrived home from work.

As a child, I spent a lot of time at Dad's furniture store, or just "the store" as we referred to it. Most days during the school year, Dad dispatched one of his two deliverymen, Robert or Reeves, to pick me up from school and transport me to the store, where I would do homework, play in the

At age two, with my mother on vacation in North Carolina

(Personal collection of Dan Emmett)

large area of the rug department, or watch the newest Philco black-and-white TVs while enjoying a ten-cent Coke until it was time to go home.

The old building that housed Emmett Furniture was built in the 1920s and constantly smelled of new furniture and fresh floor wax. There were always a lot of interesting people coming and going, including policemen, local politicians, businessmen, and just about anyone you could think of. Dad was a friend of Congressman Phil Landrum from our Ninth Congressional District, and one day as I sat watching cartoons, he appeared. This was during the early 1960s, when constituents generally held congressmen in high esteem, and I recall feeling very special as this important man sat and talked with me for a few minutes.

Other days I would be dropped off from school by one of Dad's men at the public library, where my mother worked part-time. There I would do homework and immerse myself in books about World War II or anything else I could find related to the military. Considered cute at the time, I was fussed over by Mom's coworkers, who loved to give me dinner-spoiling treats and seemed to delight in patting me on my blond crew-cut head.

I attended Enota Elementary School, where each day we diligently studied reading, writing, arithmetic, and American history as it actually occurred, all under the careful scrutiny of our teachers. We also unashamedly and with no reservation recited the Lord's Prayer during morning devotional, along with Bible verses and the pledge of allegiance. No one refused to join in any of these activities, and there were no complaints from any parent about the curriculum of hard academics, God, and patriotism.

At recess, we cultivated a healthy competitive spirit by playing a variety of violent and potentially injurious games, including tackle football with no pads and dodgeball, now banned in many schools. Not everyone received trophies for every sporting activity, and those who lost in dodgeball or other sports did not seem to suffer from permanent physical injury or lack of self-esteem.

Like most children of circa 1963, many of my relatives were military veterans from World War II or Korea. Dad's World War II service had included helping liberate the Philippines from the Japanese. Like most World War II veterans, he spoke little of his military exploits, but when he did, I listened, totally fascinated. Uncle Olan had been an army tank commander who in 1943 was captured by the Germans in North Africa and spent the remainder of the war as a POW, emerging from captivity a broken man. Two other uncles, Fletcher and Bud, served in the European Theater of Operations (ETO) and barely survived the experience.

Due to the constant exposure of being around military veterans, combined with a sense of adventure and patriotism that seemed built-in at birth, I always felt it was my duty, my destiny, in fact, to serve America, as had my father and uncles. It was simply assumed by most of my relatives that when my time came, I too would contribute. At the time, my future contribution was naturally assumed to be military service, and one day that would come to pass with my becoming a Marine Corps officer. But it also turned out to be a great deal more.

A Defining Moment

On Friday, November 22, 1963, I had just emerged from school and was moving down the sidewalk; probably looking very Opie Taylor-like, when someone said President Kennedy had been shot and was dead. I dismissed the comment, as such a thing could not possibly happen.

On that day, Robert, one of Dad's deliverymen, was designated to pick me up from school and deliver me to the store for another afternoon of homework and playtime. I approached the green pickup truck with Emmett Furniture Company on the side and then climbed up into the cab, laboring under the weight of my books contained in an official military haversack. Inside the truck, I found Robert wearing, as usual, his aviator sunglasses and smoking his usual Phillies cheroot cigar.

Normally reserved in a confident way, today Robert's demeanor was different. He was obviously disturbed over something. "What's wrong, Robert?" I asked. With some degree of difficulty, he answered, "President Kennedy has been assassinated." I was not familiar with the word *assassinated* and asked for further explanation, which he provided. So it was true: President Kennedy was dead.

As Robert drove the 1962 Ford pickup on the five-minute ride from school to the store, we rode in silence, listening to the news on WDUN-

AM radio. Upon arriving, I joined many of Dad's customers gathered around the three or four televisions in the TV department and watched Walter Cronkite go over what details were known about the assassination, which had occurred in Dallas, Texas.

Dad's customers talked about possible Russian or Cuban involvement, oblivious to my presence, probably not thinking such a young boy could comprehend any of it. The mention of Russians concerned me, as I remembered the year before, when America and the world came to the brink of nuclear annihilation during the Cuban missile crisis. If the Russians had killed our president, there would certainly be war, according to those gathered around the television sets.

As the miserable November weekend progressed, my family and I watched live coverage of Kennedy's coffin arriving at Andrews Air Force Base in Maryland. Robert Kennedy, brother of the president, accompanied the casket, along with the now former First Lady Jackie Kennedy, still splattered with the blood of her late husband.

Later, on Sunday, November 24, my family and I watched as the accused presidential assassin Lee Harvey Oswald was gunned down in Dallas Police Headquarters, also on live television. Having yet to learn about the concepts of due process and guilt beyond a reasonable doubt, I remember feeling justice had been done now that the man everyone seemed to believe had killed the president was also dead.

Up until that point in the weekend, I—along with everyone else in America—was in a type of shock over the assassination and attempting to grasp the fact that John Kennedy was no longer the president of the United States. Since I had no memory of President Eisenhower, it seemed Kennedy had been president my entire life. Now he was gone. As depressing as the entire situation was, a moment was about to occur that would ultimately change my life forever.

Somewhere during the confusing and emotional events of that weekend, I viewed a photo made moments after the fatal headshot. The photo depicted Secret Service agent Clint Hill on the back of the presidential limousine attempting to protect Mrs. Kennedy and the president by shielding them with his own body. This dramatic image, which personified not only

Agent Hill's unquestionable courage and devotion to duty but also the importance of the Secret Service as an organization, is without question the largest reason behind my choice to become a Secret Service agent.

Children are indeed impressionable.

**Agent Clint Hill shielding President and Mrs.
Kennedy seconds after the shooting**

(Work in public domain; copyright expired in 1991 without renewal.)

CHAPTER 2

College, the Marine Corps, and Ronald Reagan

As the years passed, so did many career ambitions. In the end, however, two always returned. In addition to one day pursuing a career in the Secret Service, I had set the intermediate goal of becoming a commissioned officer in the US military.

I graduated from high school in 1973 and enrolled at North Georgia College, in Dahlonega, Georgia, twenty miles from my hometown. North Georgia is a military college with Army ROTC, and it seemed like a good school for me to attend since my first goal upon graduating college was to serve my country in the military. All males living on campus were required to participate in Army ROTC, which meant wearing army uniforms and learning the customs of the US Army.

In the new era of the volunteer army, recruiting commercials invited young men and women to "join the people who joined the army" and offered "today's army wants to join you." Conversely, I had seen Marine recruiting commercials and posters with men sporting very little hair that boasted of keeping its standards high and its ranks small, wanting a few good men and not promising a rose garden. The hard-nosed Marine Corps approach to recruitment intrigued me, but I had never met a Marine officer and there were none at North Georgia College. For lack of an alternative, I was by circumstance alone headed toward becoming an army officer. Most of my relatives, including Dad, had served in the army, so I felt that was good enough for me also. However, any thought of being commissioned into the US Army ended abruptly the day I met the Marine Corps selection officer for the sixth Marine Corps district of Georgia, Captain Kenneth L. Christy.

Since North Georgia was a state-supported school, recruiters from the marines were allowed to search for suitable applicants for their programs on campus. They would usually set up a place in the student center one or two days out of each quarter for interested students to come by and talk; they would also set up a time and place for students to take the Marine Corps officers' written exam. One day when the marine recruiting team led by Captain Christy was on campus, I decided to see what they had to offer. As it turned out, what they offered was an attitude and a challenge.

My first meeting with Captain Christy occurred at a motel just outside the campus, where he and his recruiting team were staying. As I pulled into the parking lot on a beautiful autumn afternoon, I found Captain Christy seated in his car.

Captain Christy stepped out of his vehicle, and I immediately realized that I was looking at what a military officer was supposed to look like. He was a little over six feet tall with large biceps, resembling a shorter version of actor Clint Walker. With a large chest created by thousands of bench press repetitions and small waist honed from thousands of miles of running combined with hundreds of thousands of sit-ups, he looked more like a model wearing a marine uniform than an actual marine. In addition to his imposing physique, he wore aviator-style prescription glasses and intentionally sported almost no hair. His perfectly tailored uniform was made complete with the addition of silver parachute wings and three rows of combat ribbons, which included a bronze star and two purple hearts from his tour in Vietnam during 1967.

After exchanging introductions, Captain Christy invited me inside the motel lobby, where we talked. After sizing me up, Captain Christy all but stated that from the looks of me, I probably could never make it through marine training and that the army might be a better choice for me. Whether he was serious about my appearance or whether his words were meant as a challenge designed for those seeking a challenge, I was sold on the marines at that point. Captain Christy smiled a bit and summoned his equally impressive gunnery sergeant, directing him to administer the officers' written test to me. If I passed, it would signal the beginning of my journey into armed military service. Four hours later, I completed the test and that night joined the Marine Corps Platoon Leaders Class program.

The Platoon Leaders Class, or PLC, was a program where college students attended Officer Candidates School during the summer at Marine Corps Base Quantico, Virginia, and then returned to college to complete their degrees. Upon completion of college, the candidate was awarded a commission as a second lieutenant in the US Marine Corps. It sounded easy, but it was a program that had proven fatal for some.

Rebellious and undisciplined since adolescence, with a resentment of authority in almost all forms, I had for some inexplicable reason just joined the most disciplined branch of the military services. Perhaps I somehow knew that I needed the type of discipline that could only be found in the marines. As the great football coach Vince Lombardi once said, "There is something in all good men that yearns for discipline." I apparently yearned for discipline and would soon learn it under the most trying of conditions.

Summer Hell

Marine Corps Platoon Leaders Class summer camp is a physically and physiologically brutal rite of passage designed to produce commissioned officers and leaders for the US Marine Corps. This period of my life was crucial in forming the person I was to become, as well as the type of Secret Service agent into which I would one day evolve.

Almost from the moment I arrived at Marine Corps Officer Candidates School, Marine Corps Base Quantico, Virginia, on June 1, 1975, every waking moment became a challenge. On most of the days that were to follow, my platoon mates and I would have taken odds that none of us would survive the summer, much less graduate from the program.

Over the next several weeks, in the humid Virginia heat that never seemed to subside and with our heads shaved to the skin, we ran five miles each morning wearing leather combat boots, while constantly being physically and verbally harassed by the staff. On Saturday mornings after physical training, we would stand motionless for hours on the asphalt parade deck under the oppressive summer sun undergoing equipment and personnel inspections, during which candidate after candidate collapsed from heat exhaustion. The word *brutal* did not begin to fully describe Marine Corps Officer Candidates School in 1975. The staff was essentially free to do practically anything short of killing a candidate in order to determine the candidate's suitability to become a Marine Corps officer, and over the years there have been occasional fatalities. Each day began at 0430, or 4:30 a.m., with physical training that has killed strong men, hospitalized many, and caused others to quit the program. The day ended at 9:00 p.m. with lights out, at which time we all slept like the dead until the lights went on again at 0430.

Staff Sergeant McLean, one of several drill instructors (DIs) assigned to our company, and our primary tormentor, threatened every day that if I and my fellow candidates did not get ourselves "unf--ked," he would personally kill us all, or worse than being killed, he would send us home well before graduation. Another DI loved to repeatedly inform the platoon that if we thought any of us were going to be allowed to serve as officers in his Marine Corps, we were all crazier than a "shit-house rat." The statement could be addressed to the platoon as a whole or individually, and while no one really had any idea of what a shit-house rat was, we knew it must be in some way worse than the standard rat.

The main curriculum consisted of Marine Corps history, drill, weapons, leadership, and tactics, combined with a never-ending physical training regimen—all conducted under the critical gaze of battle-hardened officers and enlisted instructors who evaluated us for leadership potential. The Marine Corps philosophy of leadership dictates that, above all, before a man can lead and give orders, he must first learn to follow orders. As a result of this philosophy, failure to immediately carry out orders to the letter could result in one of many possible forms of punishment being inflicted on a candidate.

One such corrective measure required a man to run around the asphalt parade deck while holding an M-14 rifle (weighing 10.32 pounds) above his head until collapsing in the summer heat, or until the DI felt that a point of instruction had been learned. If no rifles were available, a footlocker would suffice. The program was, as much as anything, a test of who could think and function effectively while pushed to the end of human endurance and who truly wanted to become Marine Corps officers.

Every other week, we participated in forced marches of up to twenty miles with only two quarts of water per man in the worst heat and humidity to be found in the United States, with full field packs, helmets, and rifles. Those who fell back or were too slow were pushed and dragged along by the drill instructors, all the while enduring the worst verbal humiliation imaginable. If a man fell back too far, he was deemed unqualified to continue training and then simply placed in one of the safety vehicles, never to be seen again.

With a total attrition rate of around 50 percent, the merciless nature of the program was partly designed to convince as many candidates as possible to drop on request (DOR), or quit. Many did give up after enduring all they could stand and were sent home. The philosophy was that if a man would quit on a run or march, he would probably quit in combat, and these types of men had to be identified and weeded out.

As bad as things were at times, the thought of quitting never at any time entered my mind. Of all things learned that summer, perhaps the existence of this trait of character was the greatest, and it would serve me well one day as a Secret Service agent, when things began to stack up in situations that tested both nerve and stamina.

As days and weeks passed, the drill instructors never let up their relentless pressure, and we were constantly reminded that being dropped from training, even on the last day with our families sitting in the graduation audience, was always a possibility. There was, of course, a method to the seemingly total madness of the drill instructors. Those of us who graduated would become Marine Corps officers and in the future possibly be in command of our enlisted instructors. Each of these instructors wanted to be certain we were competent to one day lead them under the worst of conditions, and they went to great lengths to make certain we were up to the task.

As the training became more vicious with each passing day, and with our ranks continuing to dwindle, one thing was always noticeable to everyone: no matter the undertaking, whether it was a twenty-mile hike or five-mile run in boots, Staff Sergeant McLean along with our other DIs and officers always participated in these events, leading from the front. None ever commanded us to do anything they could not or would not do themselves. This trait of leadership, known as "leadership by example," was one of the main lessons hammered into our very souls during that hard summer by our seemingly callous mentors. I would take such lessons with me throughout life and my Secret Service career.

Then one Friday afternoon, when it seemed as if everyone were on the verge of physical collapse, the ordeal ended, and those of us who had survived stood at graduation on the same parade deck where so much misery had been endured, almost in disbelief that we had made it. We had begun with over six hundred candidates and finished with 321. I came in at 118. Final class rankings were based on three main areas: physical fitness, academics, and leadership. While my final ranking was not numerically superior, even the man who finished last, at 321, had much to be proud of.

I was, of course, thrilled to graduate, but amazed—stunned in fact—that I finished in the top half of my class. There was really no way to know conclusively how well or poorly you were doing in the program until it was all over, as there was no positive reinforcement of any type during the entire trial. At graduation, Staff Sergeant McLean shook hands with me, and then smiled the first smile I had ever seen on his face as he congratulated me on finally getting myself "unf--ked." It was a day never to be forgotten, and I have not.

Marine Corps Officer Candidates School was my first experience in a world where a man was expected to do his job and do it well, and yet there would be no accolades given. Graduation was the reward, and doing one's job was simply expected. With the hell that was Marine Corps Officer Candidates School now behind me, I headed back to air-conditioning, cold beer, civilization, and the remainder of college.

I completed college with a degree in criminal justice, and on August 19, 1977, realized the long-sought-after goal of being commissioned as a second lieutenant in the United States Marine Corps. As I stood in my summer service alpha uniform, taking the oath of office of a commissioned officer as administered by Major James Birch, I could scarcely believe it. The entire day was a blur, and after working for so many years to attain this seemingly impossible goal, I felt it was all happening to someone else while I merely observed.

When I awoke the following morning with a more-than-severe hangover from the previous evening's celebration and viewed my uniform strewn about, the realization began to set in that I was now a Marine Corps officer. After completing the Basic School and the Infantry Officers Course, I proudly served four years on active duty, most of it with Second Battalion, Ninth Marine Regiment at Camp Pendleton, California, and was honorably discharged with the rank of captain.

During my service in the Marine Corps as a rifle platoon commander, weapons platoon commander, and company executive officer, I was placed in command of thirty-eight to 180 enlisted marines, where I put into use all traits and skills of leadership taught by my drill instructors and officers at OCS. As a leader I was certainly a work in progress, but I had learned above all else that the leadership principle of "leadership by example" was perhaps the most important principle of all. If a man leads from the front, others will invariably follow. This was to become a critical part of my leadership inventory in the years to come as a Secret Service agent, where I would be responsible for leading other agents while protecting the president of the United States.

Ronald Reagan

During most of my active duty obligation including the final months, I was stationed at Camp Pendleton, California. While I had enjoyed my marine experience, I felt I had paid my dues to America for the time being and decided to leave the marines when my obligation was up in November 1981. That decision was confirmed on March 30, 1981. I had just come in from a five-mile run with my marines when the news on the radio in our company office announced that President Reagan had been shot outside the Washington Hilton.

With the attempt on President Reagan's life and my military service coming to a close, I became focused once again on my never-forgotten childhood ambition of becoming a Secret Service agent. The only problem was I had absolutely no idea how to go about it. But I was a marine officer, and even after I put my uniforms away would be a marine officer for the remainder of my life. As always, I would not give up and would somehow find a way to achieve my goal.

The Marine Experience in Retrospect

With no war while I was on active duty, all that can really be said about my Marine Corps service is that I served and that I got a lot more out of the Marine Corps than it got from me. It had taught me things that one cannot learn in school and was the granite foundation on which all things to follow in my life, such as the Secret Service, would be built. This foundation never cracked or collapsed. I have no reservations about stating I owe everything in my life, from my family to the house I live in, to God and the United States Marine Corps.

Marine Corps Officer Candidates School Quantico, Virginia, Kilo Company, Second Platoon, July 1975. I am standing second row from the bottom, sixth man from the right. Staff Sergeant McLean is bottom row, far right.

(Courtesy, United States Marine Corps)

As a first lieutenant home on leave, December 1979

(Personal collection of Dan Emmett)

CHAPTER 3

Never Give Up Unless You Are Dead

November 19, 1981, found me at the wheel of my 1978 Camaro leaving Camp Pendleton, California, in a hurry and bound for Georgia at the highest rate of speed I could manage without being arrested or killed. My luck ran out in Mississippi, when a young trooper who showed no mercy stopped me and was not the least impressed that I was a marine officer returning home from four years of active duty. He was polite and professional as he handed me the ticket.

Upon arriving back in my hometown and establishing temporary residence at my parents' home, I began the quest of attempting to apply for the position of special agent, United States Secret Service, with absolutely zero success. This enterprise of becoming a Secret Service agent was becoming a great deal more difficult than I had originally thought, and for months no one in the Secret Service Atlanta field office would return my calls. You practically had to know someone in the organization to even get in the door for an interview, and I knew no one.

Then one slow day in the summer of 1982, I called the Atlanta Secret Service office for the fourth or fifth time in as many months and asked to speak to an agent. The secretary, as usual, asked what it was in reference to. Having learned from my mistake of actually declaring I was interested in applying for the position of special agent, I stated that I would only discuss the matter with an agent. Fearful I was a psycho who might want to hurt the president or some other thing she could get into trouble for, she connected me with the duty agent. After learning of my motive in calling, he became in a hurry to dismiss me by saying the Secret Service was not hiring and probably would not be for some time.

Rather than saying, "Thank you for your time, sir," I continued to keep the hapless duty agent on the phone, wearing him down with questions about the Secret Service until he finally gave up and said he would send me an application, which he did. This was far too important an issue to take no for an answer, and I would not. The Marines Corps had taught me, among many other things, that when an objective cannot be taken one way, find another, but never give up unless you are dead.

I completed the paperwork, sent it in, and waited. After several weeks, the office manager called and informed me that the special agent in charge wished to interview me for an agent's position. My persistence had paid off. I was at least going to be afforded the chance for an interview, and it was now up to me to capitalize on this opportunity, which was apparently offered to very few.

At the appointed time and date, I appeared in the Atlanta office for my interview with Special Agent in Charge Jerry Kivett. As I sat in the waiting area of the field office, the realization came to me that this was without doubt one of the most important days in my life and I had best not botch it.

I was escorted into Mr. Kivett's office by the office manager and sweated in my seat after trying to give the firmest handshake I could muster. I then quickly offered a silent prayer I did not stumble over words or make a poor impression on this man, who now held my career future and dreams from my youth in his hands.

Mr. Kivett was something of a Secret Service legend. With only a short amount of time in the organization, he was assigned to Vice President Lyndon Johnson, soon to be President Johnson, on November 22, 1963, and was aboard Air Force One when LBJ took the oath of office to become the president of the United States. Mr. Kivett was a hard, no-nonsense man who could intimidate with a mere look. Much like my Marine Corps drill instructors, Mr. Kivett did not give the impression he possessed a sense of humor or that he ever smiled.

Mr. Kivett came directly to the point, which was no surprise to me. While burning holes in me with his stare, he asked, "So, Dan, why do you want to become a Secret Service agent?" I gave the best answer I could muster, beginning with the childhood memory of Clint Hill on President Kennedy's limo in Dallas and how the image had created a lasting impression. From there I continued to speak but have no recollection of what I said. After continuing to stare at me for what seemed like minutes, he asked if I had seen the footage of President Reagan being shot, along with the Secret Service agent who was protecting him. "Yes, sir," I answered. He then asked if I thought I could do what the agent did when he placed himself in the path of the bullet meant for President Reagan.

I recall thinking for a moment and then saying something to the effect that "the Secret Service must have a great training program. From my past experience in the marines, I know I respond well to training. While I hope I will never be placed in the position of the agent who was shot, I am confident I would respond according to training."

Mr. Kivett's face then turned into a slightly pleasant expression, and he said, "That is a very good answer." I was seated before a man who had been in President Kennedy's motorcade in Dallas on November 22, 1963, a man who had been under fire during the assassination of a president, a man who understood better than anyone what being a Secret Service agent really meant. Had I incorrectly answered his question, meaning given almost any other response than I did, there is no doubt he would have simply sent me to the door leading out of the office. Instead, he sent me to the office next door to be interviewed by Mr. Robert Coates, Assistant Special Agent in Charge (ASAIC) of the Atlanta Field Office, for round two.

Attired in a three-piece suit minus the jacket, Mr. Coates was in his late forties, balding, and just as intimidating as Mr. Kivett, but less formal. After practically ordering me to sit, he continued the quest to determine my true motives for wanting to become a Secret Service agent.

It became readily apparent to me that these men did not like to waste time. Mr. Coates, like Mr. Kivett, quickly came to the point and asked,

"Are you looking for a job?" I stated, "No, sir, I am looking for a career in federal law enforcement."

Both men's questions were designed to weed out the grossly unfit candidates. Mr. Kivett's were aimed at spotting the head case who wanted to die protecting the president and become famous. Mr. Coates's question was designed to identify the person just looking for a neat-sounding job, with no serious thoughts of what being a Secret Service agent really meant. There were other questions from Mr. Coates regarding my background and some designed to test my knowledge of the Secret Service. Then the initial interviews with these hard men from the "old school" ended, and I was on my way home, where I would wait for the next phase in the selection process, assuming there was to be another phase. While I felt I had done the best I could, I had no idea if my best had been good enough.

A couple of weeks later, I was called again by the office manager in the Atlanta office and was told that Mr. Kivett had selected me to take the written exam for the position of special agent. The test was known as the Treasury Enforcement Agents Exam, or TEA for short. It was a difficult test designed to test vocabulary, reading comprehension skills, observation skills, and for some unknown reason, the ability to do what I considered very complicated math word problems. I took the test with four other applicants and was informed later I was the only one who passed, scoring a 73 out of a possible 100, with 70 being the passing grade. For the first time since my application, I became optimistic that I might just get in.

Months passed with no word from the Atlanta office. Then one day with no warning, I was requested by telephone to appear back in Atlanta for the panel interview phase of the selection process. The panel was one of the last major hurdles to be cleared in the selection process and consisted of three senior agents, each of whom asked the candidate a long series of questions over an extended period of time.

When I arrived for the panel interview, I was escorted to the office of Robert F. Coates, now the special agent in charge, having replaced Mr. Kivett after his recent retirement from over twenty years of dedicated service to America.

Mr. Coates began the panel interview by asking the same question as he had in the initial interview months earlier: "Are you out looking for a job?" My answer was the same as before. "No, sir, I am looking for a career in federal law enforcement." He then passed the questioning over to the other two agents, Grady Askew and Buster Williams, who spent the next several hours asking questions dealing with my Marine Corps service, experience with weapons, contact sports I had played in school, my workout routine, any illegal activities I might have been involved in, my willingness to relocate if hired, and a myriad of hypothetical situations for my opinion as to a course of action.

After returning home that evening, I thought I was doing the right thing by writing Mr. Coates a note thanking him for his time and the interview. A book I had recently read concerning job interview etiquette had plainly stated it was considered totally appropriate and expected for a person to send a thank-you note to anyone who had afforded him or her an interview.

Days later, I was at my parents' house when the phone rang, and I answered it. The voice on the other end said, "This is Bobby Coates from the Secret Service. May I speak to Dan Emmett, please?" I replied, "This is Dan Emmett, sir." Mr. Coates said, "I got your thank-you note, and we don't go in for that sort of thing at the Secret Service." He continued that he was thanked by the government twice a month, meaning each time he was paid. At that point, I felt my chances of becoming a Secret Service agent were zero, and I thought his next words would be that I was no longer under consideration. After a pause for effect, he said, "Come on down to the office and pick up your background information forms," and then the line went dead. I traveled back to Atlanta that day, picked up the papers as directed, completed them in record time, and returned them to the Atlanta field office. Then the wait began in earnest.

To pay the bills while awaiting the decision of the Secret Service, I worked as a management trainee at First Atlanta Bank for the sum of $17,000 per year. Even in 1983, this was a pretty dismal salary, considering I had been making over $25,000 per year at the time I left the Marine Corps.

One day in early April 1983, as I sat at my desk waiting for the clock to announce that it was time to end the latest agonizing session of boredom,

24

my phone rang. I stared at the ringing black object for a bit before picking up the receiver. The voice on the other end of the line was SAIC Robert F. Coates.

Mr. Coates, in his now familiar and as always impatient-sounding voice, stated that he had a job for me as a GS-5 in Charlotte, base salary $13,000 per year. He directed me to take a few minutes and call him back with an answer. I immediately said, "I accept the offer, sir." Mr. Coates then gave three possible report dates and informed me that I would have to pay for my own move to Charlotte. Since I owned virtually nothing, this presented no problem. I took the first available report date of May 16, 1983.

Just as the news of my new job—new life really—was delivered at exactly the moment I needed it most, the weather in Atlanta turned from cold and miserable to warm and sunny. The only problem I now had was being so excited about having survived what had seemed an impossible undertaking that I found it almost impossible to sleep at night, or even in the day, when taking a nap would have been the thing to do. In my world, being selected to become a Secret Service agent was better than winning the lottery, and my mind was constantly racing with possibilities. This was the dream of a lifetime, and I was about to live that dream. Also, a lingering fear begin to creep in that this was all somehow a mistake and that I would receive another call from Mr. Coates telling me there was another hiring freeze, a budget cut, or something else that would ruin this dream that had its beginning twenty years earlier.

One morning in late April the phone rang. When I heard the voice on the other end identify himself as a Mr. Osborne, from Secret Service headquarters, personnel division, my stomach rolled over. He said he called to first apologize for bringing me on as a GS-5 instead of the usual GS-7, but that there was nothing he could do about that. He wanted to confirm I was to report to Charlotte on May 16 at 0830 and gave me some information about the office, such as the name of the special agent in charge. He congratulated me on being selected and wished me luck. That night for the first time in days, I was finally able to sleep.

CHAPTER 4

The Charlotte Field Office

On Monday, May 16, 1983, I appeared at the front door of the Charlotte Field Office, United States Secret Service, for my first day as a special agent. I wore a gray pinstripe suit recently purchased from JCPenney and presented as a gift from my parents. As one might expect, I had slept little the night before. It was just prior to 8:30 a.m., and no one answered when I pushed the buzzer at a door located at the end of a short hallway. Finally, at 8:35 a.m., a man who resembled the actor Robert Conrad, dressed in a blue sports jacket and gray slacks, appeared from the elevator bank just outside the office. He looked at me and asked if he could help, as he placed a strange-looking key in the door of the office. I said, "Hi, I am Dan Emmett, first day on the job." The seasoned-looking agent offered his hand and introduced himself as Paul Albergine, and then invited me in and directed me to take a seat.

Pat Pressley, the office manager, then arrived. She was matronly and friendly, while at the same time possessing a hard appearance giving the impression she took no static from anyone. Pat had worked for the Secret Service since the 1950s and knew everything there was to know about administration within the organization. She had also seen every new agent to walk through the door at Charlotte for the past thirty years. In terms of the Secret Service, she had quite literally seen it all.

Pat escorted me across the hall to the office of Bill Williamson, special agent in charge. SAIC Williamson had been in the Secret Service for twenty years and looked it. A marathon runner, he was fifty years old but looked older, with squinting Lloyd Bridges-type eyes and graying hair around the temples.

After introductions and a very short round of small talk, SAIC Williamson directed me to remain standing and hold up my right hand in order that I might be sworn in as an employee and special agent of the Secret Service. I was familiar with the words, as it was the exact same oath of office I took as a marine officer seven years earlier.

After my swearing in, which lasted less than one a minute, SAIC Williamson, as expected, briefed me on things in general, including his philosophy of good agent work ethic. He then lectured me on a topic that came as a total surprise.

Booze, Broads, and Buicks

SAIC Williamson informed me the fastest way for an agent to get into trouble was by violating the three Bs: booze, broads, and Buicks. Roughly translated, this meant combining alcohol with women and the government car.

Each Secret Service agent in a field office was given a government car to use not only while working, but also to take home at night. This benefit of the job was known as "home to work," and the Secret Service was one of the few agencies that had it. Home to work was a tremendous privilege, and the rules were clear: no use of the car was authorized other than for official business, which included going directly from home to work and work to home. No one was allowed to ride in the car other than on official business. No children, no wife, no stopping at the grocery store, dry cleaners, or bars. Mr. Williamson tied it all together by relating that, while circumstances sometimes necessitated the bending of these rules, never ever combine all three of the Bs into one event. By this he meant going out for drinks and then driving the government car with an unauthorized passenger, such as a woman. He ended the briefing by stating that any misuse of the government car, or the "G-ride" as it was known, meant an automatic thirty-day suspension without pay.

While Williamson's lecture was simple and to the point and I understood his stern, fatherly presentation, I was baffled by the necessity of it. The impression I always had of the Secret Service was that it was a highly conservative organization, with little drinking or socializing. I was about to discover that the Secret Service of the early 1980s, while devoted totally to accomplishing whatever mission was assigned and publicly presenting an image of total conservatism, was also a very socially outgoing agency. During off-duty hours, an agent was expected to have a healthy appetite for socializing, where bending the "three Bs" was expected to occur from time to time. Williamson's lecture had been a warning, and if a man chose to violate the rules, he did so at his own peril, having been sufficiently warned.

The next morning, after being introduced to the daily ritual of morning coffee in the downstairs coffee shop, run by a very nice old man named George, I was introduced to agent Frank Hancock. Frank was one of the office firearms instructors and was given the job of taking me that day to the Charlotte Police Academy, with the hope of getting me qualified with the Smith and Wesson .357 Magnum revolver, which was standard issue for the service at the time.

Frank was somewhat of an icon, or perhaps relic. He was in all likelihood the oldest living GS-12 in the service. Frank had done his protection time with President Eisenhower two decades earlier and related stories of walking the golf course with Ike at Burning Tree Golf Club with a Thompson submachine gun in a golf bag. Most agents with his time in were at least at the GS-13 level, but Frank was not a career climber. With his trademark pipe constantly clinched in his teeth, he marched to his own drummer and did not seem to worry about promotions.

Frank was known around the service as "Possum." I never asked why, but later figured it out on my own. In addition to being the most senior GS-12 in the Secret Service, Frank was also the slowest-moving agent in the Secret Service.

Possum politely asked me about my background and generally made small talk while he drove us to the firearms range in his government car later that morning. After arriving at the range, we proceeded to the appointed area used by the Secret Service for firearms training. I sat for at least fifteen minutes while Frank patiently explained the basic principles of shooting handguns. He went over grip, sight alignment, sight picture, stance, breathing, and trigger control. I had been taught all of these things in the marines until I could recite them verbatim but respectfully listened to the old sage.

Frank then explained the course of fire on which I had to qualify and then allowed me to dry fire the weapon, meaning cycle it with no ammunition to get the feel of the revolver. After a few minutes, Frank produced live ammunition and allowed me to try my luck.

I qualified on my first attempt, with a score of 290 out of a possible 300. Frank was very pleased with me and with himself. I did not offer that I had been the top shooter with the .45 pistol in my marine unit before leaving active duty. I liked Frank and had no problem with letting him believe it was his instruction that had carried the day. All organizations need men like Possum, and all new guys should listen to them.

Satisfied I was competent to at least carry a gun, Frank handed the weapon to me along with twelve rounds of .38 special +P+ ammunition, a holster, and one speed loader, which carried an additional six cartridges. I was now armed and dangerous, although probably more so to myself than anyone else. While obviously proficient in the use of a weapon, I had yet to receive any instruction on the legalities of when I could and could not use it.

The following week, the entire Charlotte field office, including the smaller satellite offices of Wilmington and Raleigh, converged on the same police range Possum had used to check me out on the revolver the week before. The purpose of this gathering was for the mandatory quarterly firearms requalification for all agents in the state of North Carolina. I easily qualified with the Uzi submachine gun, Remington twelve-gauge shotgun, and my trusty revolver.

At the end of the training day, I hooked up with Paul, the agent I met on my first day, and we headed for his road district of Western North Carolina for some basic criminal investigative work. It was a part of the on-the-job training (OJT), where a new agent was passed around from senior agent to senior agent, who would show him how things worked.

Paul and I arrived in his district during the late afternoon. We checked into our respective hotel rooms, where we would live for the next three days, and then met at the bar to plan the evening's activities, which included my introduction to the covert world of how to bend the three Bs a bit when necessary without repercussion.

The next morning I met Paul for breakfast and then hit the road for a day of check forgery investigations. It did not take long for me to realize that I did not like check forgery investigations. When a government check is stolen, the payee's signature is forged on the reverse, and it is then cashed, it becomes a federal violation investigated by the Secret Service. Today these investigations are largely extinct due to direct deposit, but in 1983, they made up the majority of investigations conducted by the Secret Service.

Check thieves and forgers are some of the lowest forms of human life. They steal Social Security checks of the elderly and income tax refund checks that are sorely needed by the recipients, and are generally involved in a variety of crimes ranging from petty to violent. Check theft and forgery often occurred in the worst parts of any city or so far out in the hills you had no radio contact with anyone.

In the mountains of North Carolina, you were totally on your own and frequently worked alone. Many of the people who lived in extreme rural North Carolina did not recognize federal law and had no regard for an agent's power under that law. While an agent had total legal authority to be on a person's property in order to ask that person to cooperate in an investigation, many of those who needed to be interviewed looked upon an agent's presence as trespassing. Investigating federal crimes in rural America was as dangerous as working in a large city, and it was easy to imagine that an agent could be made to disappear in this setting, never to be found.

Paul and I worked on four different cases, mostly interviewing payees that lived in some of the worst conditions imaginable in America. Every home we entered smelled of stale urine, and each seemed to have an army of mongrel dogs that guarded the mobile home or shack resided in by the payee.

As much as I disliked these investigations, I soon realized check cases were the main activity in a small office like Charlotte. If I was to ever get to the presidential detail, I had to do them and do them well. But agent school was coming soon, and I would be, for at least the time being, delivered from these less-than-glamorous investigations.

CHAPTER 5

Special Agent Training

The new Secret Service agent trainee attends two schools in order to be qualified to work investigations and protection in the Secret Service.

The first school a newly hired agent attends is the Criminal Investigative Training Program (CITP), located in Brunswick, Georgia, at the Federal Law Enforcement Training Center (FLETC). There, a new agent learns the basics of being a criminal investigator, common to all agents in all federal law enforcement agencies.

After graduation from CITP, the new Secret Service agent attends the second phase of his or her training at the Secret Service Special Agent Training Course (SATC), held at the James J. Rowley Training Center in Laurel, Maryland, and in my era, also at 1310 L Street, Washington, DC. There, the new agent learns about providing executive protection, as well as investigations specific to the Secret Service, such as counterfeit and check forgery. The student also (much to my delight) spends a lot of time shooting revolvers, shotguns, and Uzi submachine guns.

Like most police agencies, the Secret Service through the years has had its share of changes in training doctrine and philosophy, which seem to vary with each new director. These variances have run from a very laid-back atmosphere to an almost military boot camp environment.

In 1983, agent training really amounted to not much more than an orientation for the new agent. The philosophy was that a new agent merely had to be given the basics of the job in training; mentors and working agents in the field offices, some of whom had been on the job for over twenty years, would handle the rest. In later years, with massive retirements of the old guard, the philosophy reversed itself. With few senior agents remaining to teach the new ones coming on, training school began to become much more demanding and difficult. In my time as a student, however, my class was on fraternity row, as well as a first-name basis with most of our instructors.

Still, management let it be known that any of us could be sent home at anytime with absolutely no warning or explanation, and that we were under constant evaluation. Given the amount of rope reeled out by the service, some students did come dangerously close to hanging themselves at times.

The most intense part of our training and one of the areas that had to be passed in order to graduate and be retained as an agent was firearms. All in my class were supercompetitive alpha males, and there was no such thing as a relaxed day of shooting. In any course of fire, whether it was with the revolver, submachine gun, or shotgun, we all tried our best to outdo each other, with the loser buying the beer at our next social outing, which usually occurred that evening.

Secret Service Uniformed Division firearms instructors provide this firearms training and are arguably the finest firearms instructors in the world. Each is an expert in the use of all weapons utilized by the Secret Service, as well as possessing the ability to convey this expertise to others. In some cases, this is no small feat, as some new trainees have never fired a weapon, while others possess so many bad traits and habits they almost have to be trained from scratch.

Instructors Made of Iron and Instructors Who Threw Iron

We had a number of instructors tasked with shaping us into agents, with each having his own area of expertise and approach to teaching. Our primary hand-to-hand combat instructor was into competitive martial arts and a very different sort of guy—strange in fact. He had broken his fingers numerous times, with two or three digits still pointing at odd angles, and he delighted at times in being the object of a demonstration. He seemed to love pain.

One such demonstration included having another instructor kick him full force in the groin; he would display zero emotion and no change in facial expression. As a result of his unique talent for ignoring pain, we referred to him as "Iron Balls," but of course never where he could hear us.

Most, but not all, of these instructors were fun, outgoing people, including the somewhat demented, at times, hand-to-hand instructor. One instructor, who did not fall into the category of even approachable, much less fun, enjoyed throwing a cast-iron replica of a handgun at the head of any student he did not feel was paying attention. Usually the student saw it coming and knocked the gun down or caught it.

One day, however, a student really was not paying attention as the instructor let fly with the training weapon, striking the unaware student squarely in the head and nearly knocking him unconscious and drawing considerable blood. The instructor looked at my bleeding classmate, who was beginning to resemble a case from the ER, and spelled his name for the student in case he wanted to file a complaint. This was 1983 in an all-male class of former cops and military men. Even if my friend had required stitches and hospitalization, which fortunately he did not, there would have been no complaint.

Elevators and Dislocated Joints

Everyone in my class enjoyed life a great deal, and there was always something fun going on, usually at someone's expense. One morning the class was sitting around the mat room or practicing various holds on each other while waiting for our sadomasochistic instructor to arrive.

Without warning, I was seized by three of my classmates, who handcuffed my ankles together as well as my hands behind me. We had been practicing handcuffing, and I was duped into believing it was practice until I was being carried like a freshly slain deer toward the elevator banks. Upon reaching the elevator, my classmates lowered my PT shorts to my knees and threw me into the elevator after pushing the buttons for all floors. Keep in mind this was a main Secret Service building, where many people worked and rode the elevators each morning. Just before the door closed, my pals picked me up again, and this time delivered me to the women's locker room, where I was unceremoniously dumped to the floor amid several female Secret Service employees in various stages of undress. Upon hearing screams of disapproval, my classmates returned to retrieve me, and I was delivered to the mat room and released in time for class as if nothing had occurred. In those days, this was considered good, clean fun, and no complaints were lodged.

During the same session, while practicing a counter to a rear chokehold, I dislocated the elbow of my partner, who happened to have been one of my morning assailants. There was an audible pop heard by all in the mat room, he went pale, and his elbow was not in the place where it should have been. He was taken to George Washington Hospital, where his elbow was relocated to its normal place, and then he returned to training. Controversy still swirls about the issue as to whether or not I intentionally popped my friend's elbow.

The Formal Follow-Up

In the old days of protection, the Secret Service employed the use of formal follow-ups, which were positioned behind the presidential limousine. These were Cadillac sedans heavily modified with running boards, handrails, and convertible tops. Up until circa 1990 or so, almost all formal follow-ups were a version of this, and the shift usually rode with the top down if weather permitted. Upon slowing down and preparing for arrival, the shift would climb out onto the running boards while holding onto the handrails for a fast jump to the ground, where they could quickly surround the limo. It was the most impressive looking thing the Presidential Protective Division (PPD) did publicly, and every new agent could not wait to try it.

Prior to the state-of-the-art drivers training now at the Rowley Training Center, all vehicle training was conducted at a nearby abandoned airstrip used by the Office of Strategic Services (OSS), predecessor to the CIA during World War II. This was the setting for our formal follow-up training. The strip was a paved runway about 3,500 feet long. It had not been used for the purpose it was intended in decades, but provided a perfect place to run cars at full speed for thirty seconds or so.

Richard was our instructor for the day, had recently come to training from PPD, and was more than a bit of a wild man. The exercise began with Richard demonstrating to the class on a stationary follow-up how to mount the running boards, which foot went up first, and how to hold onto the handrails. He then demonstrated how to get off the boards safely. It was then time for us to do it for real.

We assumed that Richard was going to simply drive up and down the old OSS runway at a slow speed a few times just to give us an idea of what the whole experience was like and to provide a basic familiarization. This was not the case.

Richard was behind the wheel and at first moved out slowly with four agents walking next to the follow-up and some inside for the ride. As the car gained speed, the agents walking alongside jumped on the boards in the prescribed manner and held on as Richard put the accelerator to the floor until he easily hit sixty miles per hour.

Approaching the end of the landing strip, Richard began to slow down in order to make a 180-degree turn and speed to the other end. As he turned left with tires squealing, the agents on the right-hand side were holding onto the rails with all their strength as Richard accelerated and the centrifugal force pushed to the outside of the turn. Then Rich sped flat-out to the other end of the runway, where he would decelerate and turn this time to the other side, nearly flinging off the students on the left side of the car, who were now holding on white-knuckled, hoping not to lose their grip. Richard gave each carful of students several runs up and down the strip until he was convinced every agent knew how to work the formal follow-up. Like most of SATC, the exercise was a tremendous amount of fun, but we were all glad to be alive at the end of the day.

After eight weeks, graduation day finally arrived. Graduation was held in a small room at 1310 L Street, Washington, which barely accommodated the class of twenty-four and the small audience. Graduations from SATC are now gigantic productions accommodating over two hundred people and go on for an hour or so. In 1983 it lasted about fifteen minutes. I recall the deputy director of the Secret Service made the commencement speech but I do not recall anything more, as our class had enjoyed a vigorous graduation party the night before. With the presenting of diplomas, it was time to bid farewell to my friends and think about heading back to Charlotte.

CHAPTER 6

Back to Charlotte

On Halloween night 1983, I returned to my apartment in Charlotte from SATC, having now completed all required training to be a full-fledged agent. I was both exhausted and thrilled. It was the end of October, and I was still buzzing from all that had happened in the six short months since Bobby Coates had called offering me a job. In spite of the fact that training had been a great deal of fun, I needed some rest badly and slept most of the weekend.

The next Monday, I reported back to the office ready to go back to work. One of the first things that happened upon return was that my friend Mike Fife and I, along with another agent, Ron Lewis, all of us rookies, were sent to Atlanta to work at an event for President Reagan. Atlanta was always a good town to visit, and since this was our first protective assignment since graduation, we were very enthusiastic. Even though we knew it would only be post standing at some obscure location in the general vicinity of President Reagan, it was still protection.

We arrived in Atlanta and checked into our hotel, where all the out-of-district agents were staying, and immediately began to run into old friends from SATC. The first official activity was to attend the agent briefing. This is a gathering, usually in a hotel ballroom or conference room, where the advance team from the presidential detail briefs all agents assigned to help with the visit. Each member of the advance team is introduced, and the itinerary of POTUS (the president of the United States) is read. Each agent is then given general instructions regarding the event, including where and when to report the next day.

After the agent briefing, which lasted about an hour, we proceeded to the hotel bar, where we began to mentally prepare for our next day's assignments. Mr. Coates, the SAIC of Atlanta, was there, and I said hello to him, careful not to thank him for hiring me, remembering the verbal beating I had received a year earlier for my thank-you note. He asked me how the job was going, and I let him know it was going very well.

It was also on this trip to Atlanta that I saw what would change my immediate career goal from getting to PPD as soon as possible to another assignment instead. My assignment for the visit was standing post in the hotel garage to ensure no one placed an explosive charge in the area. While there, I saw five very fit-looking agents sitting in a Mercury station wagon with M-16 rifles and semiautomatic pistols. This was a Secret Service Counter Assault Team (CAT).

CAT is one of the special teams of the Secret Service and is comprised of agents whose mission it is to respond with speed, surprise, and violence of action against organized attacks against the president. I had heard about CAT but knew little about the program, as it was fairly new and was practically classified at the time.

I walked over to the Mercury for a better look, and started a conversation with the agent in the rear of the station wagon. He was also a former marine, and after I talked to him for a few minutes, I was so impressed that I decided that CAT was where I wanted to go next in my career after my assignment in Charlotte ended. The CAT agent handed me a piece of paper that was like an application of sorts for the program, and told me to fill it out when I got back to Charlotte and send it back to him.

While talking to the CAT agent in Atlanta, it did not come up in the conversation that an agent had to be at least a GS-9 before applying to the program. I was a GS-5 and would not attain the grade of GS-9 for two more years. CAT would have to wait for the time being, but it was without doubt the next thing on my career scope.

Campaign 1984 and Temporary Protection Assignments: Senator Ted Kennedy

One of the main functions of a field agent, in addition to conducting investigations, is performing temporary protective assignments. During the closing days of the 1984 presidential campaign, I received such an assignment, and it was to be one of the most memorable times of my career.

The president of the United States may assign Secret Service protection to anyone he wishes. An example of someone who did not rate protection by law but received it by presidential directive was Senator Ted Kennedy in 1984. This type of detail is comprised of agents from various field offices like Charlotte.

During the final thirty days of the 1984 presidential campaign, Kennedy went on the campaign trail for Democratic nominee Walter Mondale, who was washed away in a landslide victory by Ronald Reagan. Since Ted was the last of Joseph and Rose Kennedy's sons still living, two having met their fates as the result of assassins' bullets and one blown into vapor during World War II, President Reagan signed an order during October 1984 granting Kennedy Secret Service protection until the end of the campaign.

Just over a year out of agent school and still assigned to the Charlotte office, I was selected for this temporary detail and was happy to be on the road for what turned out to be a very interesting thirty days with the senator. Of the fifteen agents selected for this assignment, almost everyone was similar to me, probably by design. We were all young, male, single, and did not care how many days the assignment lasted.

It was a tough routine that only the young could have endured, working thirty straight days with no days off and visiting several cities a day. It was also my first experience waking up in a dark hotel room with zero idea of what city or state I was in, with the feeling of total sensory deprivation. It was as if a large part of my memory had been totally erased. This phenomenon would occur many times over the next twenty years as I woke up in hundreds of hotel rooms around the world, having to force myself to remember where I was and more importantly what time I had to be ready for work.

Ted Kennedy was an excellent protectee who knew how we worked and what his responsibilities as a protectee were. He always told us what he intended to do before he did it, making our job of protecting him much easier. He had been around the Secret Service since 1960, when JFK was elected president, and had been assigned a Secret Service detail of his own in 1980, when he unsuccessfully ran against incumbent Jimmy Carter for the Democratic nomination for president. He knew what we would and would not do on his behalf, and an example of this understanding occurred early in the assignment.

One evening the entire entourage had just arrived at the home of a former senator in Malibu, California, where Ted would remain overnight with several associates. People were milling about trying to get organized and find luggage and so forth when a woman turned to me and directed, not asked, that I carry her suitcase into the house. This was not going to happen under any set of circumstances. Secret Service agents never carry luggage for anyone, and to be not asked but ordered by this person to do so was, from an agent's perspective, totally vulgar.

As I stood silently staring at this person, formulating a response that would not result in my being sent home from the assignment, Ted intervened. In his best Kennedy dialect, he said, "Err ah, the agents don't carry bags." Then, someone who was actually paid to do such things appeared, and the source of my annoyance disappeared along with her bags. The agents don't carry bags. Damned right. We will die for our protectees if necessary, but don't ask us to carry bags. It was reassuring to see that Ted knew and respected this.

Hollywood Nights

During this assignment, we spent several days in Los Angeles and Hollywood, where Senator Kennedy attended a never-ending series of parties hosted by the Hollywood elite.

It occurred to me, after attending these parties night after night and seeing the same famous faces at each event, that when actors are not working on a film, their main pastime is attending parties. Some of these functions lasted well into the early morning hours, and one had to be impressed by the stamina displayed by these icons of the screen. Actor Warren Beatty was obviously not working at the time, because he seemed to be at every function the senator attended and delighted in being as close to Kennedy as possible.

As famous as these actors were, many seemed more interested in sipping a martini while talking to an agent than associating with their fellow actors. Sometimes their interest made it difficult to do our work of keeping an eye on the senator, as we stood surrounded by a group of actors each taking turns asking questions about the Secret Service. Almost all had a Secret Service anecdote each felt compelled to share with us, some going back to the JFK era.

Character actor Richard Anderson, who played Oscar Goldman on the *Six Million Dollar Man,* always seemed to get a kick out of offering to make all of us bionic. Robert Wagner (RJ) never talked to us, but would nod a cool, knowing look our way as he passed by. RJ was always the epitome of Hollywood cool as he held the obligatory drink and cigarette of an older movie star. Sinatra was more outgoing and loved referring to us as "those Secret Service cats."

One evening I was standing post outside the senator's hotel room door with strict orders to allow no one to enter, when actor Gregory Peck appeared. There was to be a party in the senator's suite, and Mr. Peck was an invited guest, although he was early. He was tall, and his persona was identical to the one portrayed on the screen. As he looked at me saying nothing while smiling pleasantly, I felt as if I were standing before General MacArthur, or perhaps Captain Ahab. I said, "Good evening, Mr. Peck," and knocked on the door to the suite, allowing him to enter. I was not going to make General MacArthur wait to see Ted Kennedy.

Fear of Flying

Because many of the towns we visited were small, we flew almost everywhere on compact, twin-engine aircraft. I had earned a pilot's license in 1982 and had flown a great deal in the marines—mostly in the rear end of helicopters that practically defied the laws of aerodynamics they were so old and worn-out. Many were a testament to the old saying "If you put a powerful enough engine on a brick, it will fly." These little planes Ted and we Secret Service agents flew in did not scare me; it always gave me a feeling of great adventure to be in one. You just never knew what would happen.

At twenty-nine, I had not yet experienced the epiphany of mortality. Ted, on the other hand, had personally seen the light coming on in 1964, when a small plane in which he was a passenger crashed, killing several on board and breaking his back. Ted was in traction and rehabilitation for months, and as a result hated flying, at least in small airplanes. It seemed to be a continuation of the "Kennedy curse," where in the case of airplanes, one of his sisters, Kathleen, had been killed in a crash in 1948, as had his brother Joe in World War II as a naval aviator.

Each of these planes we flew in was, in most cases, a private charter, complete with a flight attendant who was always coincidentally very attractive. Upon entry into the aircraft, Ted would always order the obligatory Stoli vodka and tonic, which I suppose helped alleviate his hatred of powered flight.

On one memorable occasion, we had the great experience to fly in a DC-3 operated by Provincetown Boston Airlines (PBA) from Boston to Hyannis, Massachusetts. The DC-3 was an aviation classic, the last one being built in 1946, and was one of the greatest airplanes ever flown. It was the mainstay of all commercial airlines from the late 1930s until the late 1940s, and it was quite a thrill to fly in one of these historical old beauties before they were all sent to the boneyard.

On this day, the weather was terrible, with low clouds, rain, and a lot of turbulence. As we flew onward in our intrepid DC-3 through black clouds heavy with rain that streamed down the windows, and a ride too rough for cabin service, I noticed from my left side window that, in addition to rain, there was a steady stream of oil running down the cowling of the old radial engine. I was not alarmed, as I knew all of these old engines leaked something but were still safe. It was when they stopped leaking that you had to worry, because it meant the engine was out of whatever fluid was being swept into the slipstream.

Realizing how much Senator Kennedy hated flying, and especially in this type of weather, I turned and observed him seated two rows behind me staring at the seat in front of him with his normal reddish complexion now a ghostly shade of pale. He looked up at me and I gave him a reassuring smile he did not return, at which time he resumed his staring contest with the seat.

After descending through solid dark-gray cloud cover and then breaking out over Hyannis at about a thousand feet, the pilot put us in the landing pattern and then expertly squeaked the tires on the Hyannis runway. Upon shutting down the engines, the door with ladder included was lowered, and before any of us could unstrap, Ted was moving down the aisle and off the airplane. We quickly moved after him, wondering why he was in such a great hurry and where he was headed without his Secret Service detail.

As we entered the tiny terminal, we saw his destination: the bar. Soon, fortified after his latest flying adventure, he moved to the waiting cars. The senator had also been sitting on the left side of the plane and had no doubt seen the stream of oil being blown back across the cowling, in addition to the evil-looking weather. It was in similar weather that he had crashed twenty years earlier and was nearly killed.

One of our most memorable aviation occurrences happened while on the ground. Our shift of four agents, the senator, and the senator's son Patrick had boarded a twin Cessna and just strapped into our seats when the nose of the aircraft began to ever so slowly pitch up, as if we were already in the air. With a discomforting metallic thud, the tail settled on the tarmac like a model plane without the clay counterweight in the nose. The problem was, of course, that we were still sitting stationary on the ground, with the engines stopped. Everyone could not help but laugh—everyone, that is, except the senator, who found no humor in our predicament.

The two pilots, not yet in the plane, stuck their heads in and politely asked that the heaviest of us move to the front of the aircraft. Ted was by far the heaviest, but he liked the rear seat and no one was going to tell him to unstrap and move forward. We four agents changed seating, and with the added weight of the pilot and copilot, the airplane began to pitch downward until the nose gear once again found its proper place on the ground. With the balance of the airplane now corrected, we took off without incident.

Walking Through a Time Warp

On the final day of our assignment, Senator Kennedy hosted a party at the Kennedy compound in Hyannis Port, Massachusetts, for his Secret Service detail.

The senator appeared at the festivities dressed in a blue denim shirt with a black warm-up jacket and displayed a shock of disheveled, graying hair that had not seen a stylist in several weeks. This was a drastic departure from his usual appearance over the past month, where his daily attire was a perfectly tailored Brooks Brothers suit.

While cordial, the senator was always somewhat reserved around his Secret Service detail, but with the assignment now over, he became the perfect host as he encouraged each of us to have more lobster and beer. Most of us needed no encouragement.

Late in the afternoon, Kennedy moved among his few remaining agents, offering the tour of his brother's house. As I was helping myself to another beer, I heard the senator ask, in the unmistakable dialect that seemed unique to the Kennedy family alone, "How about you, Dan?" I looked up from the beer keg, nodded, and replied, "Yes, sir, thank you, I would enjoy seeing the president's home."

As one of fifteen agents on the detail, it came as a surprise he knew my name, although perhaps it should not have. It has been reported that the senator's brother, John Kennedy, had known the names of each agent on his protective detail.

Most of the agents were forced to decline the invitation due to the offer coming late in the day, when almost everyone was preparing to fly back to their own homes after an absence of one month. I, too, had afternoon flight arrangements but decided to cancel them. I could fly back to my field office virtually anytime I wished, but what the senator was offering would never be offered again.

During the short walk to the home of JFK, the senator casually explained that the house was largely in the same condition as when President Kennedy sometimes lived there. By this, I thought he was referring to the furniture and drapes. While this was partially the case, I soon realized the senator was referring to a great deal more.

I expected the senator to provide a brief escort through the home, but instead, he handed me the key and left. Although only fifty-two years old, the senator moved back toward the main house with the posture and gait of a much older man. It was clear that the passing of the years since the assassinations of his brothers, President Kennedy and Bobby Kennedy, had done little to relieve his pain. He was still grieving. During my time with him, he also seemed a man tormented by the other tragedies that had occurred in his life.

Alone now in President Kennedy's bedroom, which darkened by the minute in the fading afternoon light, I felt for the house key in my pocket and prepared to conclude my self-guided tour. As I turned to go, something glittered in a ray of waning sunlight on the dresser and stopped me in my tracks: a set of gold cuff links.

The cuff links seemed to be waiting, like the house itself, for their owner to return. But who was their owner? As I moved closer, with my vision adjusting to the near darkness of the room, I surveyed the two gold accessories. Curiosity then turned into quiet amazement. As I moved my head inches away from the objects, I could see the letter J, then squinting made out an F, and then the letter K. JFK. The owner of these mysterious, lone cuff links had no doubt been President John F. Kennedy.

Although any number of possibilities existed as to how and why these artifacts in 1984 were lying on President Kennedy's dresser, it did not seem an unreasonable assumption, given the undisturbed state of other items in the house, that these heirlooms had been resting on the dresser since 1963. That possibility alone was a bit unnerving, not to mention the presence of the cuff links themselves.

As I started to pick one up for closer examination, my hand abruptly halted, as if grasped by an unseen force. These cuff links were perhaps last touched by President Kennedy himself; I did not feel I should be the next to touch them.

In addition to entrusting the Secret Service with his life, Senator Kennedy had also trusted each of us to merely tour the home, not touch items probably considered sacred to him. The handling of these treasures would have been totally unprofessional. I was not a tourist left to run amok in the president's home, but a Secret Service agent trained from the first day of my career to respect the personal lives and property of those I protected. As with all other objects I encountered in the home of President Kennedy, these two items were left undisturbed where they lay.

A draft of cold air moving through the house reminded me it was time to go. Leaving the cuff links in their resting place, I exited the house through the same door I had entered, and then locked it on the way out per the senator's direction. After a brief search for the senator to return the key, I discovered him walking along the beach in front of the compound.

When I handed him the key, he said, "Thank you, Dan, I appreciate your work and that of the Secret Service very much."

"Thank you, Senator, for allowing us the honor of viewing the president's home," I responded.

We talked for a few minutes, with him politely asking me things such as where I was from and how long I had been a Secret Service agent. Feeling more comfortable with the senator and with the assignment now over, I almost asked about the cuff links. Not certain, however, if he would appreciate the range of liberty I had taken with the tour, I elected not to raise the subject. After a pause in the conversation, I sensed he wanted to be alone. We shook hands, and I left him standing on the beach staring out at the ocean, seemingly looking for something or someone. I then walked to the command post, formerly the home of his other assassinated brother, Bobby Kennedy, gathered my gear, and called a cab, which would take me to the airport, where I would board an airplane for the trip home.

An Unexpected Change of Direction

It was now 1986. After three years as an agent in Charlotte, with my desire to transfer to CAT well known, SAIC Williamson brought me into his office one day and delivered some excellent news. "Dan," he said, "it looks like you are going to be in the first CAT class in 1987."

"Thank you, sir," I said and left his office practically without my feet touching the ground. CAT was growing and needed agents, who were preferably military veterans. It was time to now do what I came to do when I joined the Secret Service, which, of course, was to protect the president

**With Senator Kennedy at Hyannis Port,
Massachusetts, on Election Day 1984**

(Personal collection of Dan Emmett)

of the United States. As with many plans in the Secret Service, this one did not work out the way I intended.

One morning in the late spring of 1986, I had just arrived at work and was sitting at my desk planning the day's activities, which included report writing, lunch, and running a few miles, followed by an hour in the weight room. Something seemed different today, however. Everyone seemed distant—as if they knew something I did not. Something was up, and I sensed it had to do with me.

As I sat at my desk looking over a check forgery case, the SAIC, Mr. Williamson, came in and said he wanted to see me in his office.

Upon entering his office, I sat down in the same chair I had sat in three years earlier on my first day as a Secret Service agent. Bill Williamson sat behind his desk, appearing to almost take cover there, and wasted no time in stating his purpose. He said, "Dan, you are being transferred, but it is unfortunately not to CAT." He looked down at his desk with his hands folded, seemingly unable or unwilling to look me in the eye.

I asked, "Okay, where to then?"

Without looking up, he said, "New York."

It took a few seconds for the words to sink in. In addition to this transfer being unexpected, having previously been to New York on temporary assignments, I was well aware that it was a large, dirty, noisy, and above all highly expensive place to live. I had absolutely no interest in being transferred there. After regaining my internal composure, I asked, "What has changed so dramatically that I am being pulled from CAT and sent to New York?"

Without really answering the question, he stated that Secret Service headquarters had selected me for the assignment, and that while it was not what I wanted, it would be good for my career. As he finished with his speech, he looked up at me seeming to expect a response of some sort and asked if I had any questions.

I answered no and asked if that would be all. As I stood to leave, I said, "It might be a good idea to get someone else on deck; I am not at all certain I will take the transfer." I saw the confusion and near panic on his face. I suppose he expected me to respond to the news in any number of ways, but not to threaten resignation.

I walked out of SAIC Williamson's office to find the hallway lined with coworkers looking at me as if I had been on death row and was walking toward the gas chamber. I almost expected someone to say "dead man walking." All faces of my peer group were filled with survivor's guilt and fear. Each was sorry I was going to New York, but all were glad it was not them, and all were now terrified it would be them next time around. For more than one, it would be.

While I never had any intention of resigning, I put off signing my paperwork as long as possible, since it would officially launch me to the New York office. Each day, Bob Jones, my first-level supervisor, would call me into his office, where my transfer papers sat on the desk awaiting my signature. Each day I told him I had not yet decided whether I was going or not and then left his office without signing. Everyone was becoming more and more uncomfortable by the day over the whole thing, including SAIC Williamson. New York needed bodies for some very specific reasons and I was to be one of those bodies, but I was not ready to play the game just yet. Everyone was nervous because if I did not go, someone else would have to.

Finally, on the last day possible before being threatened with disciplinary action, I signed the transfer paper, which began the sixty-day countdown for my transfer to the office of investigations, New York. As I signed the piece of paper acknowledging my receipt of orders, I did not realize that while the New York experience would ultimately do absolutely nothing for my career, contrary to Mr. Williamson's assertion, it would become one of the many defining points in my life.

CHAPTER 7

The New York Field Office

New York Field Office: a bottomless black hole of despair that knows no limits.
—Author unknown

Upon receiving a T-number, or transfer number, an agent who has been selected to relocate to another assignment in a different geographical area is entitled to a ten-day house-hunting trip to the new region.

After overcoming the initial shock of receiving orders to New York, rather than CAT, I began to get my affairs in order, including planning my house-hunting trip. The Charlotte assistant to the special agent in charge, Lou Alfaro, who had served on PPD, was very clear about it. He said to me one day, "Dan, they screwed you, so screw them back." What he meant was that I should do whatever I wanted to do in preparation for my move and not worry about my casework. I was not so interested in screwing the Secret Service, but I was in a bit of a panic about where I was going to live in the New York area on my salary.

Looking for a Home
I had just been promoted from GS-9 to GS-11 and had little money. This was a time before government geographical cost of living increases, and

51

an agent working in the high-cost area of New York made the exact same salary as an agent in Charlotte. I was pretty broke, to say the least, and the farther away from New York you drove, the lower the rent became. Having no money for a down payment, I would be a renter, rather than a homeowner.

In June 1986, I boarded an airplane in Charlotte bound for Newark, New Jersey, and my house-hunting trip, where I would search for an apartment to live in for the foreseeable future. Upon landing in Newark, I picked up my rental car and headed south on the New Jersey turnpike. The first priority was to find a place to live for the next ten days.

After some searching, I finally found a room at a dump of a Holiday Inn about sixty-five miles south of New York for five dollars more per day than my per diem allowed. This trip was actually going to cost me money unless I gave up eating.

By the time I settled into my new reduced set of circumstances at the Holiday Inn, it was too late to do any apartment searching. With nothing now on the agenda and a bit stressed out from my trip, I had three choices: work out, nap, or go to the motel bar. I elected to have some beers and take a few hours to plan my next move.

As I sat in the bar on this very hot New Jersey afternoon, the TV was on, as they usually are in bars. This was, of course, decades before flat screens and high definition. This entire motel, however, including the bar TV, was not even circa 1980s or 70s, but rather circa 1960s. The TV was black and white, with a picture of a ghostly quality that resembled the live picture of Neil Armstrong walking on the moon. As the bartender manually turned the channel knob, not a remote, he stopped on a station covering President Reagan's trip to Glassboro State College in Glassboro, New Jersey. I had heard of the place, as two of my marine buddies, Keith Kelly and Doug Pettit, had gone to school there. While watching President Reagan and studying my beer, I decided the next day to search for an apartment in the town of Plainsboro, New Jersey, where I knew other agents lived.

Plainsboro was a very small, very old New Jersey town just a few miles out of Princeton and sat next to exit 8A off the New Jersey Turnpike. There were only two apartment complexes in town, but both were fairly new. The one I selected only had two stories, but had a view of a golf course and a bar in the golf course clubhouse that was pretty nice.

I selected an apartment on the top floor overlooking a fairway, paid my first and last months' rent as a deposit, and went on my way. I now at least knew where I was going to live, and I still had eight days left on my trip to look around. I decided that the following morning I would, just for fun, drive from my motel into New York and try to find the field office. Having never driven into New York City, I was expecting an exciting adventure and was not disappointed.

The New Jersey Turnpike

On the morning of my first New York adventure, I merged onto the New Jersey Turnpike, a six-lane highway of unprecedented danger that would take me into the canyons of Manhattan. My commute to New York would be fifty-five miles one way, taking over ninety minutes to complete, as opposed to the Charlotte commute of one half mile and three minutes.

As I headed north, I was concerned about how fast traffic was moving and how close. Everyone was driving at least seventy-five to eighty miles per hour, with scarcely more than one car length between them. I had driven many mornings through Atlanta rush hour, as well as Boston and Los Angeles, and was not new to this type of situation. I was, however, now part of morning rush hour like no other in the United States and felt as if I had no more control over the situation than if I were being swept over Niagara Falls in a barrel.

As I drove on, I wondered how this type of driving could be done with no crashes, and the answer was it could not be. Beginning that morning and almost every morning I drove on the turnpike, there was a horrific crash that was quickly pushed or dragged to the side of the road with total expertise, sometimes with limp, lifeless bodies still inside the twisted wreckage. Amazingly, there was seldom a long backup of traffic, no matter what the crash scene. These were turnpike veterans, who drove in this ballet of asphalted death every day. To them, it was no issue to see such carnage, and rather than stop and look at the scene, they merely stared ahead and droned on to their destinations. I soon discovered this seeming lack of concern for their fellow man was one of many survival mechanisms needed to get through a normal day in New York. In time, I would soon become as jaded to all of it as my fellow commuters.

One hour later, as I exited the New Jersey Turnpike and headed toward Manhattan and the Lincoln Tunnel, I came up over a rise in the highway that afforded a tremendous view of the skyline of the West Side of New York.

The panoramic view of Manhattan seemed to stretch into eternity, and upon entering the darkness of the Lincoln Tunnel, I noticed cars were moving at speeds almost equal to the turnpike. Like the turnpike, there were also sometimes accidents in the tunnels that were always catastrophic during rush hour. If an accident occurred, a special vehicle with a bulldozer-like padded blade on the front, entered from the opposite end of the tunnel and pushed the stalled car or the wreckage out of the tunnel, where it could be dealt with later.

After surviving my first trip through the Lincoln Tunnel and finding my way to the West Side Highway, I headed south toward the World Trade Center, swept along in the tide of traffic. On I drove, with the Hudson River on my right and Manhattan on my left, until I saw the huge twin towers of the World Trade Center appear.

Upon seeing a sign announcing Trade Center parking, I began my descent into parking garage hell. Down I descended, level after level, into the bowels of the Trade Center, until I reached the Secret Service parking garage, only to find it was … locked. This was New York, not Charlotte, and the garage was completely surrounded by a chain link fence with a locked gate. I sat at the gate for a few minutes until another car appeared behind me and then exited my vehicle and introduced myself to the occupants, who would soon be colleagues. When I told them where I was from and that I had been transferred to New York, they both roared with laughter, and one said, "Damn, Dan, who did you piss off to get transferred to New York?"

Most agents in New York were from the local area, and it was uncommon at that time for anyone to transfer in from outside the region. One agent exited his car and opened the gate, at which time we both drove in. An agent said, "Leave the keys in your car." I parked, left the keys in the ignition, and bravely accompanied my new comrades up to the office. In order to get to the office from the garage, one first proceeded to the main lobby of number two World Trade Center via elevator. Then one transferred to an up escalator, and then to another elevator, which deposited the traveler in front of number six World Trade Center, home of the New York Field Office. It literally took longer to get from the garage to the office than it did to travel from my Charlotte home to my old field office.

I spent the day touring the office and exploring the vast World Trade Center complex. It was like a city within a city, much of it underground. There were restaurants, banks, bars, stores, and pathway tubes—subway-like vehicles that ran under the Hudson River and came out on the other side in Jersey City. The vastness of it all was a true wonder, but in a short amount of time, it would all seem strangely normal.

A week later, I returned to Charlotte from my New York adventure, cleaned up my remaining cases, and on a molten hot day in August 1986 climbed into my Porsche 911 and then headed north to my New Jersey apartment and my new life.

After the eleven-hour trip from Charlotte to New Jersey, I moved into my apartment, which took all of about one hour. Upon opening the door to the refrigerator, I was pleased to find a bottle of champagne, vintage last month, a welcome gift from the girls in the rental office. I spent the remainder of the evening indulging in my housewarming gift and listened to a Sinatra concert on the radio. Sitting in a dark apartment in New Jersey drinking cheap champagne, for some reason, seemed very New York-like and oddly, very natural.

The following Monday, I checked into the New York Field Office for my first day of work. One of the first things I saw upon entering the office that morning was a sign taped to an agent's desk. It read: "New York Field Office, a bottomless black hole of despair that knows no limits." As I stared at the sign, I could not help but reflect on how this unexpected train wreck had occurred in my career and in the careers of sixteen other agents from around the country.

The events that led to all of our transfers to New York were really placed in motion long prior to our reporting in 1986. The reason for these transfers was that the United States Attorney (USA) for the Southern District of New York (SDNY) had lost patience with the Secret Service.

For those not familiar with the federal judicial system, the US attorney's office is the prosecutor of federal violations. In New York, a federal agent usually needed their permission to arrest a person, even though technically this was not a requirement. It was, therefore, important for an agency to have a good working relationship with the US attorney's office. During the mid-1980s, the Secret Service did not have such a relationship.

Rudolph Giuliani, the US attorney for SDNY, was a tough, by-the-book type of attorney and demanded the same of his assistant US attorneys (AUSAs). In turn, the AUSAs demanded total cooperation from all federal law enforcement agencies for which they prosecuted cases. This included the Secret Service, although the Secret Service of New York in the 1980s, especially the counterfeit squad, did not always conform to these expectations.

While the New York counterfeit squad produced results and many arrests, the US attorney did not appreciate their enthusiasm or their blatant disregard for his policies. This group of agents was made up of total nonconformist wild men who ran their own cases without asking the AUSA, "May I?"

These agents were among the die-hard investigative types. Most were scruffy, bohemian-like, and irreverent, each believing that counterfeit investigations was what the Service was all about. The squad consumed their lives. These agents were at the office or on the street seven days a week for sixteen hours a day. Few had a family life, and many had domestic issues that can occur when careers take priority over home and hearth. There was a room in the office with military bunk beds, where they slept more than in their own homes.

They were considered the elite of the New York agents, although I never saw them as being different from any other agent, aside from their willingness to live at the office, forgo any semblance of a normal family life, and do whatever was necessary to make an arrest. These agents were unique, however, in that they had pushed the envelope so hard at times and ignored the direction of the assistant US attorneys to the point that the US attorney wanted them out of New York.

Due to this conflict, it was decided that most of the New York counterfeit squad was to be transferred to offices all around the country. Ironically, some were sent to the protective details each had tried so hard to avoid.

Two months after my arrival in New York, there was a very large going-away party for the sixteen or so agents, mostly from the counterfeit squad, whom the US attorney was targeting. The going-away party for these folk heroes was held at a giant Irish bar not far from the office, whose name I now do not recall. The venue had to be big, because every agent in New York was expected to attend, all 150, plus or minus a few.

At around three thirty in the afternoon, I, along with the entire New York Field Office (NYFO), exited number six World Trade Center en route to the going-away bash. There were so many of us leaving the WTC at the same time we almost created our own rush hour. We parked anywhere there was room on the streets or in the alleys surrounding the bar and put up our police placards in the window that allowed us to park anywhere we wished. We all started filing into the bar to begin our farewell to these legends of New York. Legends they were, and all were loved by the SAIC of New York.

I had been in a lot of bars, but none came close to the size and magnitude of this place. It was enormous, like everything else in New York, and could easily accommodate our entire office. The festivities began around four o'clock and continued throughout the evening well into the early morning hours.

The special agent in charge made a speech voicing his appreciation for the soon-to-be transferred men of the counterfeit squad, especially their leader. The New York office really knew how to blow off steam, and the gathering was a great deal of fun. There was an exotic dancer hired for the occasion that tastefully plied her trade, and as the night wore on, there was a general loss of inhibitions by many. As the evening progressed, the main going-away party divided into many smaller parties, with beer-chugging and arm-wrestling contests, a couple of friendly altercations, and other diversions. When agents grew tired of one subparty, they simply moved on to another. This party made anything we ever did in Charlotte look like Mr. Rogers' neighborhood and would have caused the SAIC there to flee screaming into the night.

Investigations vs. Protection

Secret Service investigations generally center around financial crimes where there is no physical victim, other than perhaps someone's credit card being stolen and used, or a person is stuck with the loss of receiving a counterfeit twenty-dollar bill. The case can, therefore, be put into a drawer and left unattended for twenty-one days, which is the usual maximum time a field agent will spend on the road doing temporary protection, let's say on a presidential candidate. This could, for obvious reasons, not be done with murder cases, kidnappings, extortion, bank robberies, and such.

Much to the annoyance of the agents who would rather chase counterfeiters, credit card thieves, and check forgers than protect politicians, protection—not investigations—is king and always trumps investigations in importance in the Secret Service. The New York office lived in a world of its own, however, in that many agents there believed the primary job of the Service was investigation, not protection. This myth was regularly shattered when the POTUS visited New York, or when it was United Nations General Assembly time, which occurred every fall.

During United Nations General Assembly time, virtually all investigative work in New York came to a halt, due to the huge number of visiting foreign heads of state, who by law are protected by the Secret Service. Every agent from the office was used in some way to support the protective mission, and during such times, it became glaringly obvious that protection was the number one priority. The investigative-oriented agents, however, continued to insist they were real cops, that investigations were the main purpose of the Secret Service, and that agents who liked protection were mindless pretty boys.

Many of these agents liked to dress a la Don Johnson from the *Miami Vice* TV show, which was popular at the time, complete with no socks in warm weather. Having a scruffy beard, long hair, and a complete wardrobe of go-to-hell clothes was considered by these men to be their way of thumbing their noses at protection. The grungier they became, the less chance there would be of being pulled for a protective assignment.

Still, an agent in New York had to produce investigative results, and as long as an agent did, no one bothered him. The bosses realized we all worked very hard, as well as endured the unendurable beast that was the five boroughs of New York, so our taking a little personal time every now and then, including coming into work a bit late on occasion, did not bother them. In such a pressure-filled environment as New York, it had to be that way. If the bosses cracked down too hard, there would be a quiet mutiny, where no arrests would be made, so a balance had to be struck between work and relaxation. Most of the bosses in New York had started there and had a solid understanding of what it meant to be a manager in such a different place.

Not much in New York was standard issue, including the regular investigations engaged in by the Secret Service. In addition to counterfeit and credit card investigations, somehow the NYFO had also received jurisdiction over a form of telephone service theft known as "blue boxes."

Blue boxes were Texas Instrument calculators that had been reconfigured to produce telephone tones. A person attached the instrument to his or her phone line, and then using the tones that emitted the same sound as regular telephone buttons being pushed, made long-distance calls anywhere in the world for no charge, in effect, stealing service from the phone company. This was in the day when few had cell phones, and most of these criminals who were blue-box artists were from other countries. This was in some way a federal violation, and we only investigated them for the easy arrest and conviction stats they generated.

We did a lot of these cases, and they were relatively simple because a warrant was not required since a federal officer may make an arrest without a warrant for a felony in progress. The telephone company monitored the line, and when it became active, they contacted the waiting search team, and in they went, seizing the blue box and placing the owner under arrest. As I stated, the offense within itself was not one of the biggest, but the entry into areas where blue boxes flourished was dangerous. In 1984, going to a corner deli in New York was dangerous.

One warm Friday afternoon, I was preparing to go home and enjoy some time off, when the fraud squad boss came around recruiting everyone he could find to help in a blue-box takedown in the Bronx. I was single and had no plans, so I volunteered. My job was to watch the rear of the second-floor apartment where the deal was going to happen in order to respond to any items, such as evidence, that might exit the rear apartment window.

After the usual one-hour drive from the office in lower Manhattan to the Bronx, I arrived at my location in the back of the apartment building. An old chain link fence encircled this ancient, crumbling apartment complex, probably built in the early twentieth century, and the proper position for my assignment would have been inside the fence. Since that would have required scaling this rickety, rusty barrier, I elected to wait by my car outside the fence instead, not believing I would actually be needed. I picked my position and waited.

Since arriving in New York, I did not like having only a six-shot revolver, so I had taken to carrying a Beretta 92SB pistol with a twenty-round magazine. It was strictly prohibited by the Secret Service to carry any type of handgun other than the issued Smith and Wesson, although most of us did. I was alone in the middle of the Bronx and glad to have the additional security afforded by the Beretta. I also had three extra magazines, with fifteen rounds each in them. With sixty-five rounds instead of the usual six, with six more in a speed loader, I was certain not to run out of ammunition in any situation. I have always been a firm believer that there is no such thing as having too much ammunition.

I heard over my radio that the phone company confirmed the blue box was in use, and then heard that our team was in the apartment. These entries usually were over quickly, and I waited for the all clear so I could begin the voyage back to New Jersey. As I stood in this cesspool of human misery looking down at the debris, broken whiskey bottles, used condoms, and hypo needles on the ground, I watched the back of the suspect's apartment with my arms crossed, leaning against my car, not expecting anything to happen. About the time I was getting ready to get in my car to go home, the blue box came flying out of the second-story window, followed moments later by its owner.

Realizing I had to actually take action, I scaled the ancient chain link fence, tearing my best polo shirt as well as myself, and then took chase after this young speedster. I was thirty-one and in great shape, but the blue-box owner was about twenty and scared, thus making him about twice as fast as me. After climbing the fence once—not so gracefully—I had to scale it once again, chasing my target, who had gone over it like a deer. Several blocks later, in an alley, I cuffed the suspect and then did a search for weapons. After turning him over to the team, I went home to clean up my minor gash and self-medicate. Other than ruining my shirt and spilling a little blood, it was a gratifying way to end the week.

Criminals involved in stolen credit cards or counterfeit money and even blue boxes were usually involved in other things a lot more serious. While a person might not be willing to go to war over phony money, he might over drugs or a lot of genuine cash he had from ill-gotten gains. You never took anything for granted on any execution of a warrant, and we served a lot of warrants in New York.

A warrant execution team is broken down into sections, the first being the entry team. The entry team is usually comprised of the strongest agent, with a battering ram made of a large-diameter piece of storm pipe with handles welded on, and an agent armed with a short shotgun. The remainder of the team, approximately six agents, then follow.

Upon entry, the shotgun agent and the agent with the battering ram clear the rooms one by one, searching for anyone who might pose a threat. Upon finding anyone, they pass him or her back to the rest of the team, where he or she is handcuffed and detained in a central area, such as the living room. After the premises have been secured, the people taken into custody are sorted out as to who needs to be kept and who can be released. All persons are thoroughly searched, for agent safety. An agent is posted at the door to ensure no newcomers show up while a search is in progress. The entry team then reverts to helping the search team look for the things to be seized. The fun of the entry is usually over in less than two minutes, but it is pure adrenaline. You literally never know what potential threat is waiting on the other side of the door.

The Supreme Court had ruled during this era that before knocking down a door, the police had to announce their identity and purpose, and then wait a reasonable amount of time for the person to answer the door. The law could have been a large hindrance to law enforcement were it not for the fact the Supreme Court never defined what constituted a reasonable amount of time. As a result, we knocked and yelled, "Police, search warrant," and before the "t" in warrant was pronounced, the door was down and we were in. To wait any longer gave the bad guys time to get rid of any evidence they might have or, more importantly, grab a gun and kill you. When you yelled "Police," the bad guys didn't know which law you were there to enforce. Was it the blue box, or was it the pound of cocaine under the floorboards?

The execution of warrants in New York never seemed to end, and on one such occasion, I came very close to killing a young man.

The entry of the day was another blue-box case. Over time I had come to dislike these cases immensely, because the violation didn't amount to anything, but people could get hurt doing them just the same. The target this day was, as had come to be the norm, a bad section of the Bronx, which in itself is redundant.

The team formed up close to the target location, but not close enough to be detected by any possible counter surveillance, and waited for the phone company to call, telling us the line was up. Finally the call came, and we moved out to the target location. We stacked outside the door, and on the signal from the team leader, the door was breached and in we went; I wielded the shotgun.

We had become pretty smooth with these entries, as we had done so many; we were quickly moving room to room, clearing the area and finding surprised people who were totally taken off guard by our presence. We had almost finished clearing the small apartment when we came to a room with the door locked.

The battering-ram agent and I smashed the lock and made our entry to find a boy of about sixteen in bed with his right hand under a pillow. I pointed my Remington twelve-gauge shotgun at his head and chambered a round, safety off, while I shouted the standard command of, "Show me your hands." He did not look the least bit frightened but just stared with a blank expression. I repeated the command, and he began to move his hand under the pillow as if moving it toward something but did not bring it out from under. As I held the most dangerous weapon in the world for close combat on this boy's head, I could feel my right index finger move inside the trigger guard. Action is quicker than reaction, and if this boy came out with a gun—which at this point I had to assume he was about to—there would be no time to do anything other than to kill him.

I was now conscious of my breaching partner next to me pointing his revolver at this young man, who seemed determined to die on this particular day. Propped up on his left elbow, the boy began to slowly move his hand out from under the pillow. I pulled the stock tighter into my shoulder and prepared to fire. I remember moving my point of aim from his head down to his chest. For some reason, I thought that there would be less mess if I hit him center of mass rather than in the head.

Then the hand came out. There was nothing in it or anything under the pillow. As I lowered my shotgun, I exclaimed an expletive and let out a heavy sigh of relief. The young man had been asleep when we entered, with his hand under the pillow. When we breached the door, he was frozen stiff with fear, he later said to one of our Spanish-speaking agents. As it turned out, the kid was from some South American slum and spoke no English. He had no idea what I was saying, only that two Americans were pointing large guns at him, and he was too terrified to move.

We finished securing the apartment and began the search, where we found two blue boxes—one that was up and running and another one hidden. This incident reminded me of what I already knew: a million blue-box seizures were not worth the life of a person, including that of the boy I had come within a delicate trigger pull of killing. While I had functioned perfectly, making in a split-second the correct decision to not shoot, moments later, emotionally drained, I sat clutching the twelve-gauge Remington with both hands around the receiver, forehead resting on the butt of the folding stock. After a few minutes, I stood up, cleared the weapon, handed it to my team leader, and said, "See you tomorrow."

As he took possession of the Remington, he replied, "Great job today, Dan."

"Thanks," I said as I moved to my car for the two-hour trip back to New Jersey.

I went home and had a few beers, thinking of how I had come as close as a person can come to killing another human being without it having happened, and then I put it behind me and moved on. It was just another day in New York, where anything could happen at any time; and in the world of law enforcement, this incident was nothing special. What made it different was that while uniformed street cops run into this type of thing almost daily, Secret Service agents run into such situations just frequently enough to scare the total hell out of a person.

I always found it surprising that, with the number of high-risk entries we did, no one was shot during the three years I was assigned to New York. The reason was clear, however. We used the best people available and always used a lot of them. It was a simple case of overwhelming the bad guys with sheer numbers before they could react.

CAT School at Last

Two years had passed since my arrival in New York in 1986. While sitting at my desk on a Thursday, going through my investigative notes from an uneventful interview of a potential suspect on Coney Island, Assistant to the Special Agent in Charge (ATSAIC) Nick Lucas called me into his office. Lucas told me that he and everyone else knew I was interested in going to the Counter Assault Team (CAT). Then he told me the CAT school that started on Monday at the Secret Service training center in Beltsville, Maryland, was one agent short. It seemed that at the last minute, a candidate had backed out, leaving an open slot. They needed to fill it, and he asked me if I wanted to go. "Yes," I replied instantly, "I can go."

Nick asked if I was up to it physically since I had had no time to formally train for the fairly rigorous school. I replied that I had no doubts as to my physical readiness and was certain I would have no problem.

"Fine," he said, "go home and pack." I set a record that day driving from New York to my apartment in New Jersey.

CAT school was three weeks long in those days, each week consisting of six training days, with each day running about twelve hours. The school was challenging, especially in the July heat, with the hardest parts being weapons qualification and little rest and recovery time.

During this period, the standard Secret Service agent was required to qualify with a 210 out of a possible three hundred points for each issued weapon. CAT agents, on the other hand, were required to score a minimum of 270 out of a possible three hundred, or 90 percent, with the M-16 rifle, MP-5 submachine gun, and the Sig Sauer pistol.

The CAT courses of fire for these weapons incorporated almost impossible time requirements and multiple magazine changes that made the standard Secret Service courses seem quite elementary. Failure to meet qualifications with one weapons system constituted total failure. For CAT students, failure to qualify meant going home without a graduation certificate. For operational CAT agents, it meant leaving the program short of tour. In CAT, weapons proficiency was everything.

I was the first in my class to qualify with the M-16 rifle. This came as no surprise, since I was practically married to one in the Marine Corps; I was already well familiar with it. Others had difficulty, and it appeared that not all were going to make it to graduation. With the expert tutelage of the best firearms instructors in the world, however, all pulled through.

As the very long days wore on, things became more difficult as knees began to swell and elbows were rubbed raw and then became infected from firing on cement in the prone position. The school was and is dangerous, as CAT agents conduct tactical training using live ammunition and frequently fire past one another as they envelop an objective. One mistake can be fatal, and through the years, there have been many close calls, prevented from becoming fatalities only by the focused attention of the superb CAT instructors.

I was to discover that CAT was the only school in the Secret Service where students experienced what it was like to be shot at. Part of our realistic training involved all CAT students standing about three hundred yards downrange with an instructor firing an M1 Garand rifle chambered in 30.06 at an impact zone within mere feet of where we stood. The purpose of this exercise was to familiarize the CAT student with the sound of a bullet as it traveled almost directly toward him.

The bullet from a high-powered rifle travels faster than the speed of sound. Therefore, when being shot at, the first thing a person hears is not the sound of the weapon being fired, but the "crack" of the bullet, which sounds like a bullwhip as it goes supersonic. So, the sounds of being shot at by a high-powered rifle are "crack," followed by "kaboom," not just the kaboom, as most would imagine. Gary Thompson, the instructor firing the M1, was an expert rifleman, and none of us was concerned about his errantly shooting us, although Gary always delighted in putting his rounds as close to us as possible without hitting someone.

Other than Joe Clancy, who had survived plebe summer and beast barracks at West Point in 1973, none of my classmates were former military. CAT school was the most physically demanding thing they had yet to encounter, and besides Joe and me, none was accustomed to being yelled at. This was not a gentleman's school and was very paramilitary in nature. Although everyone in the class had been an agent for at least four years, we were treated by the staff as mere trainees and were constantly harassed. For me, it was like old times, although no one told me I was crazier than the enigmatic shit-house rat of Quantico lore. While others fretted and complained privately over the treatment, I took it all in stride with a smile and was just glad to be there.

While demanding, the course was elementary compared to Marine OCS, Basic school, or the infantry officer's course. The big difference was that I was twenty years old when going through marine training, with amazing powers of recovery, and now I was thirty-three. Recovery time for sore muscles was much slower, and all of us were walking like old men from the assisted living home going to bingo night by the end of the second week.

Graduation came after three weeks, and much as my drill instructors in the marines had done, these Uniformed Division instructors transformed into human beings upon our being awarded graduation diplomas. The turnover rate in the CAT training department was almost zero, and these would be the same instructors that would continue to help train us for the next several years as we became operational CAT agents.

With a CAT graduation diploma in my bag, I returned to New York to finish out what I hoped would be my last year there.

Escape from New York

The seasons changed as they always do, and it was now spring of 1989. I was becoming more restless by the day, as I had now received news from all my CAT classmates that each had reported to Washington for the beginning of their protection tours.

Then one day with no warning in late March 1989, my orders to CAT came through. I received an official teletype with a T-number, a transfer number. I had survived the survivable accident that was the New York office, and it was time to pack up and head south to Washington. As I began planning for a house-hunting trip to Washington and getting the movers lined up, Nick, my ATSAIC, approached me and asked if I had contacted the movers yet. I said I had not, and he told me to hold off. I told him what he already knew, which was that I had a T-number. My orders were official. He said the deputy special agent in charge (DSAIC) had not approved the transfer, and I was not leaving New York.

My T-number was retracted as quickly as it had appeared. I was not going anywhere for the moment and was as livid as I had ever been in my entire life. This was a petty power play by the DSAIC designed to prove a point. He was the number two man in New York, who would dictate when people would leave, and no one was going anywhere without his approval. I finally settled down, accepted the decision, and went on with my normal routine.

Two weeks later, I was surprised to receive yet another set of orders directing me to CAT. Once again there was a T-number, and it was on paper, making it official. I again prepared to get my house in order for the move, and once again Nick called me into his office to tell me the same news as before: the DSAIC had not blessed this set of orders either, and they were to be rescinded as the previous set had been. I became more than angry, practically screaming that this entire situation was more than ridiculous and someone needed to step up and challenge the issue. This was not going to happen, as Nick, a GS-14, wanted to be a GS-15, and going against the second-in-command of the New York Field Office was not the way to get it.

The next day, the DSAIC, who had rescinded my orders now on two occasions, called me into his paneled inner sanctum, which overlooked the Hudson River and was adorned with awards earned during his career as well as photos of himself alongside various presidents. Not inviting me to sit, he demanded to know whom I knew in Washington at Protective Operations, the directorate in charge of all protective details. In light of my having received not one, but two sets of orders within a month and without his approval, he was led to believe I was somehow connected to someone in Washington. I told him I knew no one, and that if I did, I wouldn't still be sitting in New York.

I suggested that the answer to the mystery of my receiving orders on two occasions was as simple as the fact that I was a CAT school graduate and CAT agents were needed to protect the president. I further suggested that all of my CAT classmates were now operational and that Protective Operations wanted to get me down to CAT before it was necessary to send me back through CAT school again for retraining. After throwing an icy stare my way, the DSAIC dismissed me with the wave of a hand and then resumed his paperwork as if I were the person who vacuumed his office. I went back to work, which on this day meant to the gym, and then headed home.

Mike, my group leader, who worked for Nick, was one of the much-loved New York investigator types. His protection time had been with Ronald Reagan Jr., and as most like him, he had no use for protection. He did, however, recognize a bad situation when he saw one. He went to the oppressive DSAIC on my behalf without really making it appear it was on my behalf and convinced him to allow me to leave New York.

Mike explained to the DSAIC that, while stepping on my orders and trying to break me might be great sport, it was damaging the morale of the entire office. Almost everyone wanted out, except perhaps the kids still living at home with their parents, and to see a man given orders and then have them practically torn up in front of him on two occasions was causing rifts within the ranks. If a man could not escape from New York even with orders, what chance did anyone have of ever getting out?

The DSAIC saw the wisdom in this and was concerned that if morale suffered, so would production, and therefore his own career. He had proven his point, however. No one went over the wall without his okay; the word had gone out that he had the muscle to stop anyone from going without that okay.

Three more weeks passed, and a third set of orders to CAT appeared bearing my name and another T-number. This time the DSAIC did not attempt to have them rescinded. I was to find out later that, even if he had tried to pull my orders again, the office of protective operations in Washington would have overruled him. I was trained to fill a position no one else could fill unless they had been to CAT school. Having run out of CAT graduates, they needed me, and now.

In August 1989, three years almost to the day after I had checked into the NYFO, I finally attended my own going-away party. It was about one-third the size of the party I had attended in 1986 for the outgoing bad boys of the counterfeit squad. There were no exotic dancers, and the SAIC and DSAIC did not attend. It was a fairly large turnout, however, and most of the people there were those I had, over the course of the past three years, drunk with, broken down doors with, suffered common hardships with, and risked all with. I would miss each of them.

At the conclusion of my going-away party, I departed New York with the Holland Tunnel in my rearview mirror for the last time. The following week, I realized the hard-won goal of moving to Washington, DC, where I would become a part of one of the most elite counterterrorist units in the world: the United States Secret Service Counter Assault Team.

CHAPTER 8

The Counter Assault Team (CAT)

Some Background

CAT, the Counter Assault Team, is the tactical unit of the Secret Service comprised of special agents whose stated mission is to neutralize organized attacks, multiple attackers, snipers from a known location, and rocket attacks against the president of the United States through the use of speed, surprise, and violence of action. The agents that comprise CAT are a very unique group of individuals and are arguably some of the best agents in the Secret Service. Each is physically hard and highly disciplined, and most delight (at times) in being politically incorrect when the opportunity presents itself. These are agents that some of the more genteel personnel in the Service feel should be locked away out of sight and released only in times of life-threatening crisis.

In addition to being iron-man fit, each is an accomplished expert with all issued weapons, as well as small unit and individual tactics. Some speak a second language, and all hold degrees in a wide range of disciplines, including accounting, engineering, and law, with more possessing advanced degrees than not. Among their ranks are pilots, combat veterans, former teachers, military officers, and noncommissioned officers. In contrast to their sometimes colorful demeanor, each also has impeccable party manners and looks immaculate in a business suit, presenting an image all would expect a Secret Service agent to portray.

Today CAT enjoys a reputation in the international law enforcement community as one of the most elite counterterrorist units in the world. In spite of this highly respected status, its beginnings were humble. Gaining acceptance in an organization such as the Secret Service, which had for years resisted the idea of an elite within an elite, was a long and painful process. The Secret Service is a very old and traditional organization, which for many years fought significant change of any sort, and for decades its mission remained essentially the same. It was a conservative, compact organization that had few missions and did them all exceptionally well, with many not seeing the need for expansion in its scope of duties.

There were many terrorist organizations in the world at the time, but none really seemed interested in hurting America or its president. As a result, the gentlemen of the Service were not overly concerned with the threat of terrorism. The old men, sometimes literally very old men, who ran the Service in those days did not feel there was a need for any sort of tactical unit within the organization. Some in the front office had been on the job since Truman or even FDR, and there was not much progressive thinking going on. Their feeling was that the agents of the Presidential Protective Division could handle anything that came along.

Consequently, since assuming its mandate to protect the president in 1901 with the assassination of President McKinley, the Service had not changed a great deal in its methods. It used more agents and now had jets and armored limos to move POTUS about, but it primarily still only trained for the lone gunman scenario or perhaps a sniper. That was the way the Service saw it, and just as the Service retained its use of revolvers until after almost every organization in law enforcement had transitioned to semiautomatic pistols, that was the way it would remain for a very long time.

While the headquarters elders saw no need for a centralized counterterrorist unit, in the late 1970s, it gave the authorization to large field offices, such as New York and Washington, to create their own versions of such a unit. These teams were field agents who worked their cases and performed normal investigative activities until a presidential visit or high-threat protectee came to their city. Then these agents would deploy in any vehicle that would hold five large agents and not embarrass the Service. The quasi-CAT car would position in the motorcade several vehicles behind the limo, to be used in the event of an organized attack on the motorcade. These early teams were known as simply the "muscle car" and were the predecessors to modern-day CAT.

The initial CAT selection course conducted at the Secret Service training center in Maryland was primitive at best and only lasted one or two weeks. Most of the training consisted of physical training and range time trying to learn the M-16 rifle. The CAT physical fitness test consisted of ten dead-hang pull-ups, either over or underhand, forty push-ups in one minute, and forty sit-ups in one minute, followed by a 1.5-mile run that had to be completed in 10:30 (ten minutes and thirty seconds) or less. After the run, the agent had to do the upper body exercises again, with the pull-ups' hand position the opposite of the first set. Failure of any one event was total failure, and the candidate would be sent home.

Some attack scenarios were conducted, but mostly consisted of Uniformed Division firearms instructors firing blanks from the woods. CAT's early weapons were Smith and Wesson revolvers augmented by Uzi submachine guns, with one M-16-wielding agent. That was the general composition, but there was no real standardization, from training to uniforms to weapons.

With no strong support from HQ for money and training, early CAT was a very haphazard affair at best. Training and focus of mission centered almost entirely on responding to an attack on a motorcade or airport tactics. There was little to no emphasis on urban deployment or countering an attack from inside of a building. Retraining was left up to the agents, for the most part, back at their field offices and was hit and miss. It was truly half-assed in every way, but it was a start and better than nothing.

The early teams, or "muscle cars," did not really have to be tactical geniuses or even good at tactics. Their real mission was to deploy in case of an attack, draw fire away from the protectees onto themselves, while the shift evacuated POTUS. If they killed any bad guys, so much the better. Their true purpose was to be sacrificed, if necessary, in order to give

POTUS time and the opportunity to escape from the kill zone. From the beginning of the program, the assignment attracted those with a sense of adventure and a seemingly total disregard for danger. There was never a shortage of volunteers.

By the 1980s, terrorist attacks around the world were on the rise, and our brethren at the FBI saw the future far better than we. In 1982, the FBI established HRT, the Hostage Rescue Team. HRT was somewhat of a SWAT team, but with a much broader mission. In addition to the centralized HRT, based out of their academy in Quantico, Virginia, they established similar but less specialized teams in the major field offices. They had the budget, personnel, and the all-important backing from FBI HQ. From the beginning, it was a first-rate operation.

Not wanting to be outdone by the FBI in this new field of counterterrorism, the Service responded by creating a new branch called the Special Programs Branch (SPB), also to be known as the Counter Assault Team (CAT). With the establishment of the Special Programs Branch, CAT had become a permanent protective assignment lasting two years on the average. The agents that comprised it would come from all over the country and be based out of Washington, with the muscle car concept now scrapped. After the two-year assignment, a CAT agent would usually move to the presidential or vice presidential details, depending on the needs of the service.

By the mid-1980s, training had improved enormously, as had weapons carried. Now everyone in CAT would have an M-16 assault rifle and the new Sig Sauer P226, 9MM pistol. Instead of six rounds like the revolver, it held sixteen rounds. In an organization that still issued revolvers to its agents, carrying a Sig was a status symbol envied by all. Only CAT carried them, adding to the mystique of the program.

Although CAT now officially existed, the proper utilization of this new resource was an enigma to supervisors, and as a result, CAT in the early years was either improperly used or not used at all. For example, CAT did not accompany the president on all movements, and its presence was at the discretion of the presidential detail supervisor running the movement. It was not uncommon for PPD (Presidential Protective Division) operations to call CAT notifying them of a POTUS movement, but CAT would not be requested. CAT was being deliberately left out when its presence didn't suit the White House bosses or its proper use was beyond the tactical knowledge of the conventional supervisor. These exclusions began to create friction between PPD and CAT.

There were several additional causes for this friction. Much of it came down to the fact that many at PPD distrusted CAT, did not feel it was needed with its massive firepower, and were ignorant of its capabilities. Things had been fine for almost a century of protection without CAT, and many felt it was not needed now. Another reason PPD did not like CAT in the early days was the freedom we enjoyed. We were totally on our own and were having entirely too much fun for some on the detail. We were an unconventional, independent lot, and almost everything we did spoke to that side of us. There was also some old-fashioned jealousy involved. On the road away from Washington, CAT began to take over from PPD the reputation of being the Secret Service social elite.

My CAT Tour Begins

I checked into CAT from New York in August 1989 and officially began protectingthe president of the United States, George Herbert Walker Bush.

On my first day, Randy Wood, the SAIC, called me into his office, where he welcomed me to CAT, congratulated me on doing so well in CAT school, and then said essentially that I was a total "new guy" (FNG) and that he did not want to even hear my voice for one full year. I was just happy to finally be in CAT and had no problem playing the role of the mute.

Randy was an army officer and paratrooper during the Vietnam War and had been an interrogator of Viet Cong and North Vietnamese captures. He could be somewhat hard and demanding in many ways, but he also gave us a great deal of freedom to do the job as we saw fit. He loved his CAT boys and would go to the wall for us with the upper management whenever any heat came our way, but he would chew the major part of our behinds off if we were wrong about something. He was a firm believer in handling discipline himself, not putting our CAT business out for the world to see, and any of us would rather have taken a major beating than

**My wife, Donnelle, and I with President George
H. W. Bush and First Lady Barbara Bush**

(Courtesy of the White House)

to be the attention of his ire. He was hard to know, but once he accepted you, he would never let you down. Above all, he was a great leader, and his men always came first.

I began my CAT career as all new arrivals do, spending the first year in the rear of the CAT truck and learning how things worked in the program. My tactical duty was to provide a base of fire for the team in the event of an attack. Unofficially my largest duty included always having my team leader Phil Hyde's personal bag available for him and stacking the gear bags of the remainder of the team, consisting of John Mrha, Mike Lee, Tom Impastato, and Ron Perrea, in a neat and accessible manner. On days when I was not scheduled to work with my team, I was at our training facility, honing my weapons skills and working out to maintain CAT-level fitness.

By my second year in CAT, I had moved up to team driver and then was selected as assistant team leader. In 1992, Randy appointed me as the team leader in command of team one, the team I had started with as a new guy three years earlier. It now consisted of a new group of agents, with the old team one agents having moved on to other assignments, either within CAT or elsewhere in the Secret Service.

During the spring of 1992, CAT was unexpectedly placed under PPD as a section, thus losing its divisional status. As a result, everyone on CAT became by default members of PPD. This change in organization was announced one day by the director of the Secret Service in an all-hands meeting, with the news not well received by either CAT or PPD. As separate entities, we got along well. Merged into one division, there were initially problems. Still, there were times when we were very popular with the non-CAT agents of PPD.

The Thirty-Eighth Parallel, Korea: Eyeball to Eyeball

As almost adversarial as the relationship could be at times between the working shift of PPD and CAT, CAT was always welcomed on certain trips, when an attack on the president was more probable than others. One such trip was to Korea with President Clinton in 1993. During this visit, President Clinton, or more likely someone on his staff, decided that he should walk on "the bridge of no return."

This bridge runs perpendicularly through the thirty-eighth parallel of latitude separating the two countries of North and South Korea and all American POWs that North Korea chose to release walked across the bridge to freedom in 1953. Since the cease-fire agreement in June 1953, the North Koreans have controlled the northern end of the bridge and the South Koreans the southern end.

On the Communist northern side of the bridge, there was an observation post occupying high ground, which overlooked the south and provided a perfect view of any activities on the bridge. This was also the exact location where axe-wielding North Korean soldiers murdered Army First Lieutenant Arthur Bonifas in 1976. The camp we operated out of during this and other trips to Korea was named in his honor.

An agreement existed between the two nations that no rifles were allowed in this area from either side, and the closest significant American forces were one mile away. Even with this agreement between the North Koreans and United Nations Forces, CAT was directed by PPD to go to the bridge and preposition where we could monitor POTUS, the bridge, and the North Korean observation post.

No one seemed to know if President Clinton grasped how potentially dangerous this stop on the bridge was. The Secret Service obviously believed this move unwise and that the president was unnecessarily risking his own life, as well as the current peaceful state of affairs on the peninsula. Nevertheless, he was POTUS and he wanted to stand on the bridge, so stand on the bridge he would.

North Korea was briefed ahead of time that POTUS would be making the stop on the bridge. This was a diplomatic as well as intelligent maneuver. The Communists would have gone quite ballistic over the sight of President Clinton and company on the bridge had they not known of it before the fact.

The night before the president's visit to the bridge, the commanding officer of Camp Bonifas, a colonel, held a dinner for all Secret Service personnel on the trip. After dinner over drinks in a secluded corner of the officers' club, the colonel, a veteran of both Vietnam and Desert Storm, put our situation in very black-and-white terms, characteristic of military men. He stated to the team, "If attacked and you survive the assault, and chances are you will not, you will be acting as a speed bump for the North Korean regulars. We have a squad of shock troops waiting just outside the DMZ who will ride to battle, but they are ten minutes away. In any case, it will be the longest ten minutes of your life …" All on the team appreciated his honesty as we accepted this warrior's offer for another round of drinks and his toast to our success and survival.

The following day, my team—consisting of agents Mike Carbone, Charlie White, Lee Fields, and Jim Cobb—finished gearing up and mounted our Humvee for the move to the bridge. We had just rolled a few yards when the voice of the command post agent and CAT school classmate Joe Clancy jolted me with its urgency. Joe's voice was usually calmer than calm, but on this occasion, the calm was accented with strain. I was aware from the tone in Joe's voice that something was wrong and already knew what it was before Joe announced it.

"Hawkeye from command post," Joe forcefully broadcast over our encrypted frequency, causing me to lower the volume on my radio. "CP from Hawkeye, go ahead," I answered. "Hawkeye from CP," Joe responded, "be advised that numerous North Korean soldiers have been observed moving into their sector of the bridge armed with AK-47 rifles." As I turned and gave my team the "I told you so" look, I keyed my microphone and simply replied back to Joe, "CP from Hawkeye, roger that."

I had anticipated this entirely predictable event well in advance; I never had any intention of letting my team go to the bridge armed with only pistols. Before we left Camp Bonifas, I had given the order to carry our full complement of arms and ammunition—pistols, M16s, and a combined total of over a thousand rounds—and I was prepared to assume full responsibility for that decision in order to provide the Secret Service with plausible deniability should the fact be discovered. In addition, I had given the order for each of my team members to carry their rifles with a round in the chamber, violating a major Secret Service regulation for long guns.

Since we were not supposed to have our M-16s to begin with, violating the round-in-the-chamber regulation was minor.

This situation was serious, damned serious, in fact, and I was not risking my team or the life of the president based on a forty-year-old agreement I had correctly predicted would be broken by the Communists. As good as we were, though, a gunfight pitting five CAT pistols against scores of Kalashnikov assault rifles would have been somewhat lopsided. Because America always plays fair, the Communists likely expected us to not have rifles, and this incorrect assumption on their part slanted the odds in our favor a bit more.

Now knowing what we were up against, we moved out to the bridge, where we found the Communists in and around their observation post arrogantly brandishing their Kalashnikov AK-47 rifles, as reported by my good friend Joe Clancy. To our Secret Service way of thinking, the only reason they would commit such a violation of the no-rifle agreement was because shooting the president of the United States is much easier with a rifle than with their Russian-provided Makarov pistols.

The terrain around the bridge, while somewhat improved since 1953, was probably much as it had been at that time. The area was a combination of dirt and asphalted road surrounded by fields and forests. The area was also mined, and it would only take driving off the beaten path a little bit to produce a big, flaming kaboom, so we moved carefully. After settling into the best position from which to deploy in case of attack, which in this case was away from the arrival point yet near enough to respond, we saw quite clearly the Koreans eyeing us with binoculars and trying to shake us up a bit by pointing riflescopes in our direction. We counter eyed them with our own binoculars, and although our M-16s were scoped, we kept our rifles low and out of sight. Unlike our North Korean nemesis, we at least had concealed our rifles, giving no indication that we were possibly in violation of the meaningless clause in the 1953 cease-fire agreement.

The North Koreans we now traded game-face looks with were not members of just any foreign military. All were the sons or grandsons of the same men who had helped kill over fifty thousand Americans from 1950 until 1953. Each from birth was indoctrinated to hate America, its form of government, and its leaders, and that resuming the war with the United States was both inevitable and desirable. The Korean War had ended in 1953 with a truce, and we were technically still at war with North Korea. If they wanted to resume the shooting war again, today would be the perfect day.

By fate and necessity, our mission of fighting a delaying action while POTUS escaped was not much less than certain death should things break bad, and the colonel in charge of the area had so much as said so. None of us had any doubt that in addition to the North Koreans in the observation post with AK-47s just yards from where the president of the United States would be standing, there were in all likelihood more in the tall grass on their side of the bridge, being eaten alive by various insects as they lay motionless.

This scenario was the quintessential example of why CAT existed and why we trained with such intensity. With a command from me that consisted of only one word, the team would be out of the vehicle and placing a heavy volume of pinpoint, accurate fire on the objective in less than four seconds. Regardless of our own fate in the seconds that would follow, we hopefully would accomplish our mission and the president of the United States would live another day. Everyone on my team knew this and accepted it as our job, and there were no complaints. We had no intentions of being mere sacrificial lambs or dying a glorious death, but we were confident that the five of us would produce many, many dead Communists if they decided to do something so ill-advised as killing an American president.

The mood in the CAT vehicle was serious and quiet, but confident as I announced our plan of action in the event of attack. Everyone nodded with grim smiles that they understood their assignments, and I had total confidence in these men that each would do his duty and respond to his training if called upon. We were brothers who worked together, trained together, traveled the world together, and now if necessary, would meet our fates together. We all shook hands and waited for the arrival of the president of the United States into what amounted to nothing less than a made-to-order "kill zone."

Then with no warning, in a release of nervous emotion, everyone in the truck began to laugh hysterically, as if the funniest joke in the world had just been told. For one brief moment, we could have been anywhere other than where we were. As we laughed like drunken fraternity boys, all mirth died as quickly as it began as we saw the approach of the president's motorcade.

At the designated time, POTUS and shift arrived at the bridge. Upon POTUS emerging from his right rear seat, he was immediately surrounded by the shift. From our position, we could see a noticeable increase in activity and movement from the North Korean observation post. If a gunfight were going to happen, it was going to happen within the next few seconds.

The shift then began doing a constant series of radio checks with us. It was becoming somewhat ridiculous as well as irritating, but they wanted to be sure we had radio contact with them in the event an attack occurred. We didn't bother pointing out that, while there would be a lot of activity in such an event, no one would be talking on the radio. Any survivors from the shift would be covering the POTUS and trying to evacuate him across the expanse of the bridge, while CAT did its best to turn the Communist observation post into a sieve and kill as many of North Korea's finest as possible.

I felt calm as the adrenaline took effect, although I could feel my heart rate increase and my grip tighten on the hand guard of my rifle concealed beneath the instrument panel. As we sat in our vehicle, we stared at the North Koreans while they stared back. Meanwhile, POTUS leisurely strolled along the bridge as if he were at Camp David, with the satisfied, relaxed look of a man with no concerns.

After walking a little farther onto the bridge than he should have, practically into North Korea, in fact, Clinton looked around the area for a few minutes and then returned to his vehicle, and we got the hell out of the zone, the totally pointless photo op ending without incident.

Training for the Worst

In order to maintain our high level of readiness, we trained constantly. If we were not protecting POTUS, we were running immediate action drills,

The Bridge of No Return, looking into North Korea. The Communist observation post is visible in the upper left-hand corner of the bridge.

(Personal collection of Dan Emmett)

on the firing range, or in the gym. As good at our work as we were, we were about to become much better due to an agent placed in charge of CAT training, named Lon Garner. Lon would take our training to new heights and set a new standard for CAT training that continues to this day.

Lon was a former Navy SEAL, and although low-key and modest as to his background, it did not take me long to realize he was without question one of the toughest men I had ever known. In addition to having been a SEAL, he was a former police officer and had ridden rodeo while in college. One of his favorite ways to relax, which always made me nauseous just to watch, was drinking Crown Royal whiskey straight up while chewing tobacco. Swimming a couple of miles each morning, along with weight training and running, kept him in top shape. He was a believer in hard mission-specific training and had spent two years in CAT himself, where I am sure he was making mental notes on how to one day better the training if he got the chance. Once placed in charge, he did that very quickly.

Through Lon's training program, our skills became as sharp as those of any police tactical unit in the world. There was, however, one problem with the training, and it had nothing to do with Lon. The problem, and one that was potentially lethal, was that CAT protected POTUS, as did the working shift, but at the time the two entities seldom if ever trained together.

In the event of an attack on POTUS, PPD shift agents had absolutely no idea what CAT was going to do or not do for them, and CAT really did not know what the shift was going to do, other than attempt to cover and evacuate POTUS, as was their job. In order to remedy this shortcoming, CAT and the PPD shift began training together regularly, and problems quickly surfaced that had to be corrected.

One of the first joint training exercises I participated in with CAT and the main presidential detail took place at Kennebunkport, Maine, at the Bush compound. President G. H. W. Bush had agreed to allow the Secret Service full access to the compound for some realistic training.

On the first problem, CAT responded to the main house, killed the attackers, and then consolidated our positions around the house. Within seconds of our securing the residence, a PPD agent ran around the corner of

My CAT team in Korea preparing to move to the Bridge of No Return. Left to right: Agents Charlie White, Jim Cobb, Mike Carbone, the author, and agent Lee Fields. That is North Korea behind the yellow line.

(Personal collection of Dan Emmett)

the house and promptly shot me with his training weapon, which fired blank ammunition. The bizarre thing was that this agent and I knew each other, and I had in large letters on my back, POLICE. In spite of this, he became so excited over the simulated attack and overcome with tunnel vision, upon seeing a man in a black outfit (me), he promptly blasted me with his Uzi.

This type of incident occurred for quite some time on a regular basis while conducting joint training at our training center in Beltsville, Maryland. It took many, many repetitions over many, many weeks and months before we could break certain members of the shift from the habit of shooting CAT agents.

The problem was really simple. Under stress, even in training, some people totally lose the ability to think clearly, and all situational awareness goes out the window. The result is the confused person shooting someone known to them, because all they see is a black uniform and a rifle. These exercises alerted us to certain agents whom we had to watch closely.

Unlike CAT agents, who had to pass a rigorous school before being allowed anywhere near the president, PPD agents were selected from the field and moved to the detail with no additional training. Due to the manpower requirements of PPD, most agents did not have many chances to train, and this shortcoming was glaring. This condition has now been largely corrected, but was a major issue during the early days of the CAT/PPD merger.

CAT Collateral Duties: Protecting the Vice President

In some cases, CAT, upon request, would accompany the vice president on high-risk trips, usually overseas.

On a trip to the Far East in 1989 in support of then Vice President Dan Quayle, my CAT team was in a motorcade en route to a planned stop, and I was working in the back of our Suburban providing rear security. I had just joined CAT about two weeks earlier, and this was my first foreign trip.

Although we had total intersection and route control, one of the many motorcycles that navigate the streets of the region had somehow gotten into the motorcade and was coming up fast behind us. The biker, who wore a backpack, was traveling parallel to the motorcade and would accelerate as if he were coming up toward the CAT truck and limo, and then back it off and drop back. It would not have been permissible to allow this interloper to pull past us and adjacent to the VP limo. Once there, the biker could damage the limo and perhaps the vice president in any number of ways.

At the approach of the motorcyclist, who this time looked as if he were going to try and move past us, Phil Hyde, my team leader, calmly turned to me and with his Boston accent said, "If he looks like he is going to go past us, take him out." As the biker began to move closer to the CAT truck, I aimed with my M-16, placing the ultra dot sight on his chest with the barrel of my weapon clearly protruding from the rear of the vehicle. Upon seeing my rifle aimed directly at what had to be him, the biker abruptly decelerated and then moved back and out of our motorcade. Who he was or if he meant to harm the VP, no one will ever know. These types of incidents seemed to happen a lot in this part of the world, mostly due to the maniacal manner of driving found there. In our work, however, we always had to assume the worst in such cases.

With the Vice President in Haiti

Sometimes the most dangerous part of being in CAT was not on the mission itself, but rather on the advance. In 1989, I was sent to Haiti to do a CAT advance for the VP, who once again was Dan Quayle.

Haiti is the poorest country in the western hemisphere, located adjacent to the Dominican Republic, south of Cuba, and can be a lawless region depending on the mood of the people. There was a great deal of political unrest during the period of the VP's visit, and things were tense from the moment of the advance team's arrival in the capital of Port-au-Prince. The airport was straight out of a bad movie, with one runway and the median strewn with the wreckage of several derelict DC-3s. The terminal building was a pockmarked reminder of other times of unrest.

Upon the arrival of the advance team in an Air Force C-141, the Department of State regional security officer (RSO) briefed us. He related that over the past several days, more than one policeman had been captured and burned alive by the criminal element of the local population. Their method of execution was to corner the officer, and after he had expended all ammunition, place a tire over his head, pinning his arms to his side, and then filling the tire with gasoline and igniting it. I was armed with a Sig Sauer P226 9MM pistol, which by then was standard CAT issue, along with five magazines of fifteen rounds each, and an M-16 rifle with 180 rounds of ammunition. After the briefing from the RSO, I carried them all.

In addition to the information regarding the human torches, the RSO stated firmly that we should never under any circumstance step outside of our vehicle while in the city of Port-au-Prince. In the event of a vehicle breakdown, we were to contact the embassy and request assistance. During this time, it was felt that any American caught on the streets could be treated to the same fate as some of their own police. I was determined not to be taken alive by these barbarians, and if cornered, would take as many with me as possible before ending the episode on my own terms, not theirs.

Each morning the advance team would get into our armored Suburban at the El Rancho hotel and drive to the embassy. In order to get there, we had to drive straight through downtown Port-au-Prince, where locals would surround our vehicle anytime we slowed down. The VP lead advance would drive, while I sat in the right front seat with my rifle, hoping the older, mechanically questionable Suburban would make it to the safety of the embassy yet again. Each morning the sight of at least one dead body lying somewhere close to the embassy or floating in the ocean would greet us. Due to the heat, it did not take long for these unfortunate souls to notify us of their presence through the sense of smell before we could see them.

On this trip in 1989, there were other dangers in addition to the restless populace. One was the anopheles mosquito. During this trip, we were warned about the malaria-carrying mosquitoes, which seemed to be everywhere and in great numbers. At night in my hotel room, which was nothing more than a small room with a cement floor, a bed, and a giant red bathtub, I slept very lightly, with a sheet wrapped up to my neck to thwart the bugs, and gripped my Sig pistol in my right hand. Sleep did not come easily with the mosquitoes and the constant sound of gunfire that could be heard all night, ranging in distance from very far to very close.

The most concerning part of the advance was a night move from the American Embassy to the airport in order to meet the Air Force cargo plane that was bringing the VP's armored cars, as well as additional agents and my CAT team. This was for all intents and purposes, for the moment, a land without law, and CAT was the only protection that could be counted on in the event we were ambushed.

We arrived at the airport without incident at about 0200, when most everyone in the area was sleeping. This was done by design in order to avoid a broad daylight spectacle of the VP's limo and follow-up being driven from the airport to the embassy, where they would be stored until his arrival in two more days.

My team came off the plane with their rifles, and we formed up a CAT team in my vehicle to protect the motorcade on the way back to the embassy and then proceeded to the hotel, where all six of us were treated like royalty by other agents sent to assist in the visit. None were shy about voicing their gratitude for our presence, and that night our bar tab was taken care of by others.

On game day, upon our arrival at the airport to await the vice president, we were pretty apprehensive about the scene that awaited us. Since our arrival the week before, we had seen virtually no police or anyone from the military. Today, however, there were at least two hundred Haitian militia armed with M1 Garand rifles surrounding the airport and walking about the tarmac area.

The M1 had been the main battle rifle of the US military from 1942 until around 1962, when it was replaced with the M14. Close to six million M1 rifles were produced, and although it only fired eight rounds of 30.06 ammunition before having to be reloaded, many nations around the world, including Haiti, were happy to receive the M1 as a gift from America. While these rifles were old and beat-up, they were very lethal.

As I wandered over for a look at these soldiers and their weapons, I noticed that some of the ammunition clipped to their rifle slings was black tipped, indicating armor-piercing ability. This was a major concern for obvious reasons. In civilized countries that were longtime allies, such as Great Britain, this would have presented no issues of concern for us. Haiti did not fall into this category, however, and so many Haitians armed with rifles with an effective range of well over five hundred yards, and ammunition that could punch through armor, was of concern.

History had taught us that even in far more civilized countries than Haiti, there was always cause to view armed military at political events with suspicion. A good example was when Egypt's president Anwar Sadat was assassinated by his own military in 1981 during an outdoor political event. America had never lost a vice president to assassination, and I was determined that today would be no different. We were taking no chances with these Haitians.

When confronted with questions regarding the addition of the armed Haitians, the Haitian government counterpart explained to the airport site agent that these last-minute troops were a "reaction force" should the airport or the motorcade be attacked. This move was not a part of the agreement with the Haitian government, but typical of how the Service sometimes finds itself duped in third-world countries like Haiti.

After all plans are agreed upon between the Secret Service advance agent and the local government, on the day of the visit they are usually not worth the paper they are written on. I always wondered if it was simply the ignorance and indifference of third-world countries, or if they just enjoyed abusing the most powerful country in the world in such situations simply because they could. An agent could argue with his foreign counterpart all he wanted in such cases, but there was little one could do when the protectee was on final approach and the formerly friendly, "no problem" counterpart all at once became an arrogant, dictatorial monster.

Days prior to a foreign visit by POTUS or VPOTUS (Vice President of the United States), if things became too heated between the host government and the Secret Service, the nuclear option was to simply tell the host government that the president or vice president would cancel the visit due to security concerns. To avoid the embarrassment of such a cancellation, the host would usually concede—until the day of the visit when it was too late for the protectee to back out, like now.

When such things happen, a good agent simply adjusts to the situation. I told the frustrated airport advance agent not to worry, that this was a situation we had seen in other countries and we would handle it.

As Air Force Two finally arrived and parked with all eyes on it, the CAT Suburban slowly and with little notice moved into a position where the so-called "reaction force" of Haitians could be observed and, if necessary, neutralized.

Although we were severely outnumbered, six highly trained CAT agents with M-16s each holding thirty rounds, with an additional thirty-round magazine clipped alongside and access to hundreds more, were certainly a match against these poorly disciplined and undoubtedly ill-trained militiamen.

We positioned ourselves in a deliberately conspicuous position so that the Haitians would know we were watching them closely. Sometimes the mere possibility of the use of force is as good as the use of force itself, and the unwanted militia behaved themselves in a quiet, docile manner, seemingly afraid to handle their rifles or even look at us.

I was told later that the Haitians were not happy about our posturing, but we couldn't have cared less. Our job was to ensure the vice president left Haiti alive, not to make friends. The diplomats could work out the hurt feelings later at the next embassy party over martinis. They had their job, and we had ours.

With the visit concluded and the VP now safely airborne en route back to Washington, the advance team formed up at the airport to await our transportation back to civilization, an old, noisy C-141 like the one we had flown in on. We sat on the tarmac under the broiling, merciless Haitian sun leaning against our gear bags until we heard the unmistakable whine of the four big jet engines that would take us out of this hellhole and back to America.

After landing, the pilot, an older major wearing the star and wreath on his wings signifying he was a command pilot, voiced some concern about the current airworthiness of his plane but said that there were no backups available. After some consultation with his copilot and flight engineer, he decided to give it a go if we were willing. We were all tremendously relieved, as all were willing to take a chance on this plane and crew rather than be left in Haiti for another night.

We boarded the plane, which had been sitting in the Haitian sun for more than an hour by then, and the interior was well over 110 degrees. After we were all seated in the stifling heat of the fuselage, the major came back to our area and announced that there was no water on board and asked if we would be willing to share whatever we had by pouring it into the cooler at the front of the passenger compartment. Not enough water in this heat was serious, and several agents were already showing signs of becoming heat casualties. No one hesitated, though, and a line formed to pour whatever water remained into the communal supply. As a result of sharing, there was enough water for all on the trip back to DC. That was one of the things about Secret Service agents. One might try and steal your date, but he would give you his last dollar, last beer, or the last of his water merely for the asking.

After stepping off the world's slowest jet and seeing home again, I was as always thankful to God for allowing me to have been born in the United States, rather than a country like the one we had just left behind. That feeling of gratitude always surfaced after returning from such countries as Haiti, and years later a place even worse than Haiti—Afghanistan.

With the Vice President in the Philippines and Korea: Neckties and Carpet-Tack Bombs

During my career, agents in general, and especially CAT people, had a pretty gregarious sense of humor, almost to the man.

Just prior to a 1989 CAT trip to the Philippines, there had been a lot of unrest among the people, and the local police to quell the violence had used a lot of tear gas. More trouble was expected. On this trip, we were supporting the VP, and Dan Quayle was due to arrive at the airport in the late evening. That night, as we stood around the CAT truck waiting for Air Force Two, a rotund, rosy-cheeked, little vice presidential staffer bashfully wandered over to our truck. He was more than a little concerned about breathing tear gas should the police throw any. It seems he had asthma.

All CAT agents had been gassed more than once, either in CAT school or in the military. It was unpleasant but no big deal, but of course, we had gas masks and staff did not. I tried to explain to the staff person that in an open area or in a motorcade, he would not even notice gas should it be deployed. He was not satisfied. I patiently explained that the wind dissipates the gas very quickly, and worst case, if he did get a whiff, it would be gone and over before he knew it. He was still not satisfied. I was trying to assuage this little man's fears as best I could, but he would not believe me. Becoming a bit exasperated, I finally said, "If they throw gas, urinate on your tie and wrap it around your face; that will protect you better than anything else." He was now satisfied.

I was puzzled as I watched the young man wander over to the jungle tree line, where he removed his tie and began relieving himself on the tie. I was astounded that he would actually do it, but after all, he had asthma. He was quite thorough in his mission and must have had to go for quite some time. He then walked past the CAT truck with a new swagger in his step, born of the confidence of the field-expedient gas mask around his neck like a bandanna. He thanked me for my help and rejoined his group, where we saw them discussing something obviously of great importance.

In a few minutes, the same jungle area was lined with male staffers relieving themselves in their ties. Each then filed past the CAT team sporting their modified neckwear. The VP landed and boarded the motorcade, and we proceeded to his next stop with no incidents of tear gas being thrown. If there had been gas, however, the vice president's staff was prepared.

On a VP trip to Korea during the same time frame of the Philippines trip, the locals had been throwing carpet-tack bombs at police, and some injuries had occurred. Essentially the bomb was not much more than a big cherry bomb wrapped in tape and carpet tacks. We were warned about them and that on the trip up to Camp Bonifas with the motorcade, where we would meet up with the VP the next day arriving by helo, we should keep the windows rolled up.

It was late at night, and we were sitting in our truck in the motorcade waiting to move north to Bonifas. The weather was warm and humid, so our driver, agent Mike Lee, had his window down for the time being to allow some air in. The cars started to move, and Mike pressed on the accelerator, at which time he started screaming, "God damn, God damn!" Phil Hyde, our team leader, turned to him and said, "Mike, calm down," and then asked what the problem was. It seems Mike's sunglasses had fallen from behind the sun visor into his lap. In the dark, he thought it was a carpet-tack bomb. When he and all of us realized what it really was, we laughed until we could not breathe. "Damn, man," he said, "I thought I was about to get my balls blown off." Mike had big balls, and we were all glad he had not lost them. We made it up to Camp Bonifas with no other incidents regarding the possibility of balls being blown off or other misfortunes; we rode with the windows up the rest of the night.

CAT Flourishes

Time moved on, and so did the never-ending flow of CAT agents to the presidential working shift, as more and more of the older agents moved out of the White House and on to other assignments. It was becoming common for almost entire shifts surrounding the president to be made up of former CAT agents, and they were all excelling. Physically hard, experts in small-unit protective tactics, and virtuosos with all issued weapons, these agents began to literally run PPD, with three of the most recent five SAICs being former CAT agents.

By the time of my retirement in 2004, CAT had come light-years since its initial inception and had become one of the most highly respected branches of the Secret Service. The truly extraordinary agents who make up CAT are a force to be reckoned with and for all Americans to be proud of. When the day comes for CAT to deploy in a live-fire situation to save the life of the president—and that day will come—I have total faith they will carry the day.

CHAPTER 9

The Agent Who Loved Me ... Eventually

During my four years assigned to the CAT team, I experienced many exciting and interesting episodes that would provide memories for a lifetime. The most important, however, was not any adventure involving the protection of the president. It was my marriage to another agent, which occurred in November 1990.

My decision to finally go down the aisle came as a shock to many, as I was a thirty-five-year-old confirmed bachelor, or so everyone—and I—believed. I had enjoyed an active social life, and the thought of marriage was something that had never really occurred to me. It was an institution I believed was meant for others, but not something I could see happening for myself.

Donnelle and I first met in November 1988, when I was assigned to the New York Field Office and was preparing to conduct motorcade advances for Mikhail and Raisa Gorbachev of Russia during their visit to New York. Proficient in the Russian language, Donnelle had been flown to New York from her post at the San Francisco Field Office to assist with the advance. Since I did not speak Russian at all, she was assigned as my interpreter to assist me in working with my KGB counterparts.

Our first meeting occurred as the result of instructions from the command center to pick up a female agent in front of the old Vista Hotel adjacent to the World Trade Center and bring her to the field office.

As I pulled up in front of the hotel, I found myself looking at what was without doubt one of the most beautiful women I had ever seen, standing on the steps of the hotel, who appeared to be waiting for someone. I dismissed the thought she could be my contact or even one of our agents, as I thought she was far too attractive and feminine.

She was tall and statuesque, over five feet ten inches, with jet-black hair, high cheekbones, and dark Italian eyes, combined with a posture and demeanor that unmistakably said she was a lady. I sat in my car staring at her, leering in fact, but realizing whoever this lovely creature was, she was totally out of my league and could only be admired from a distance, as one would admire a beautiful painting.

As I continued to stare, she stared back and then began moving down the steps of the Vista toward my car and me. She opened the door and got in, introducing herself with a perfect smile that could blind. Up close, she was even more beautiful. Over the next several days, that beauty drove me to near distraction from the business at hand of moving Russians safely around New York.

She and I worked closely together, and while I tried hard to impress her with whatever charm I could muster, she seemed totally immune and uninterested. Even so, we became friends during those few days, and when it came time for her to return to San Francisco, I sadly thought I had probably seen the last of her.

Over the course of the next year, we stayed in touch by telephone but never saw one another—that is, until I checked into CAT in 1989. As luck would have it, my first several CAT trips were to the San Francisco area, where she and I continued running into each other and began to date occasionally. With each encounter, I was beginning to feel this was someone I could actually have a lasting relationship with, although I fought the emotion, as the entire situation seemed too improbable to seriously pursue.

My affection for her began to grow, but if she shared that affection, it was not noticeable. I had noticed one thing for certain, however: this woman had the kindest eyes I had ever seen, and my will to resist a real relationship was weakening each time I looked into them.

During the late spring of 1990, she was sent from San Francisco to Washington for the purpose once again of using her Russian language skills for the visiting Russian head of state, Mikhail Gorbachev. As usual, I took up as much of her time as possible.

One evening after dinner at the Old Ebbitt Grill across from the White House, while a bit lubricated with twelve-year-old Scotch, I unexpectedly blurted out, "Hypothetically, if I were to ask you to marry me, what would you say?" She responded, "Perhaps," and that she would be in Dallas the next month assigned to protect someone I had never heard of, by the name of George W. Bush, son of the current president, George Herbert Walker Bush. If I were serious, she said, I could come there and ask her.

Apparently I was serious. In June 1990, I found myself in Dallas, Texas, holding an engagement ring while asking this Italian American beauty if she would indeed marry me. To my astonishment, she accepted. On November 10, 1990, we were married in Gainesville, Georgia, with both a Catholic priest and a Baptist minister in attendance.

After our honeymoon, we moved into my small condominium in Gaithersburg, Maryland. Because one of us was usually gone most of the time, our marriage seemed like a never-ending honeymoon or even the greatest date in the world. It is a date that has now lasted almost twenty-one years and produced the finest son anyone could wish for.

The other and best Special Agent Emmett with our son in the
White House Roosevelt Room, circa 1999. A former deputy sheriff
before joining the Secret Service, Donnelle spent twenty-one years
as an agent and served four years on PPD before retiring from
the Secret Service as an assistant special agent in charge.

(Personal collection of Dan Emmett)

CHAPTER 10

Human Shields and Operant Conditioning

It takes special types of people to willingly sacrifice their lives for that of a president, or anyone else for that matter. Yet this is exactly what all commit to the moment they take the oath of office to become a Secret Service agent.

No one ever elected to the office of the presidency was worth dying for as a person. Presidents are only people who live and breathe like anyone else, but they are worth dying for if necessary due to the office they hold. The office of the presidency must be protected at all cost. If people do not truly believe this, then the Secret Service is not the career they should pursue. In order to assure its agents will respond correctly in situations that are life-threatening to the president, the Secret Service takes dedicated people and subjects them to repetitive training until certain responses become automatic, removing thought, heroics, or cowardice from the equation.

Assassinations and attempted assassinations are usually over in less than three to four seconds. In such events, no one has time to think about what to do but rather can only react according to training. The training all agents initially receive and then continue to receive throughout their careers is a form of operant conditioning, whereby a person reacts automatically based on constant exposure to certain stimuli and events.

Agents, for example, are trained how to disarm assailants with knives and handguns. The exercise is done so many times in training that when and if an agent faces a real gun or knife, the agent will automatically attempt to disarm the person without thinking. This super-repetitive training removes any thought process associated with the reaction, and responses become totally automatic, with the mind not making the distinction whether the situation is real or training. This response must be instantaneous if such situations are to end successfully.

Such was the case on September 4, 1975, when agent Larry Buendorf, while assigned to PPD, disarmed Lynette "Squeaky" Fromme as she pointed a loaded Colt .45 semiautomatic pistol at President Gerald Ford in Sacramento, California.

While escorting President Ford on a walk to the capitol, Mr. Buendorf saw a hand come up holding a gun. Per training he sounded off, "Gun!" Then ripping the loaded Colt out of Fromme's hand in the prescribed manner, he pulled it into his chest, while the remainder of the detail evacuated President Ford to a safe location. Practiced in training hundreds of times over his career with a dummy weapon held by an instructor, this time it was a live weapon in the hand of a person intent on killing the president. Mr. Buendorf's response to the potentially lethal situation was perfect.

Secret Service agents have been accused by some shallow people, who have no clue about much of anything other than who the finalists on *American Idol* are, of being brainwashed because of their unquestioned willingness to protect the president. I totally reject the assertion that Secret Service agents have been brainwashed or that each is nothing but the Manchurian candidate or one of Pavlov's dogs responding to a signal.

It was this repeated training that saved the life of Ronald Reagan on March 30, 1981. On that day, John Hinckley, who had embedded himself inside the press pen with the media outside the Washington Hilton, fired six rounds of .22 caliber bullets at President Reagan. Of the six shots fired, four found a human target. One slug hit a Washington, DC, policeman, one hit the presidential press secretary, one hit the president after ricocheting off the limo, and one hit Secret Service agent Tim McCarthy.

The entire episode was over in less than three seconds. Even so, the sound of the sixth and last round had not finished echoing off the buildings surrounding the Washington Hilton when SAIC Jerry Parr already had pushed President Reagan into the backseat of the limo as ATSAIC Ray Shaddick covered them both while shoving them into the car and slamming the door. This was the quintessential example of operant conditioning produced by years of training, and while Pavlov's dogs might have been interested in the tires of the limo, they would have had trouble closing the door.

Based on these types of incidents and their outcomes, the validity of Secret Service training is indisputable, and the above-mentioned incidents are total proof. These agents responded to two separate incidents six years apart. All men reacted, as trained, in a nanosecond. None had time to think, only react, which they did, and perfectly. Each was a member of the Presidential Protective Division.

CHAPTER 11

The Presidential Protective Division (PPD)

When I had been in CAT four years, eighteen months of which had been as a section of PPD, I knew my time in CAT was getting short. Most agents spend no more than three years in the program, but I enjoyed the work to the extent that I stayed as long as possible.

One day while in the CAT office, I was called to the Old Executive Office Building, which housed the offices of PPD directly across West Executive Avenue from the White House. There I met with Pete Dowling, an assistant special agent in charge. Pete was tall and physically fit, with prematurely gray hair that made him look older than his years, although distinguished and authoritative. He had been one of President Clinton's agents during the campaign and had been assigned permanently to PPD after Clinton won the 1992 election. Pete was one of the few agents on the detail who had the president's ear and carried on frequent informal conversations with President Clinton.

I arrived in Pete's office early, where I sat down and waited for him. While waiting, I talked to Tommy Farrell, who had been my first boss when I arrived in New York. Tommy was now an ASAIC on PPD also, and we enjoyed talking for a few minutes about the old days in New York. Although only four years in the past, New York seemed like an eternity ago.

Upon Pete's arrival in the office, he and Tommy shared a look, and Pete said, "Dan, your time is up in CAT. Where do you want to go next?" He continued by saying, "You can have almost any assignment you want in the Secret Service."

I replied, "I want to stay on PPD and become a member of the working shift."

He smiled and said, "Okay," and that I was to report the following Monday.

With CAT now behind me and my new assignment as a shift agent on PPD a given, I had in ten years as an agent attained all major goals in my career. No matter what the future might hold, I had through planning, tenacity, and luck managed to land the prime assignments sought after by most young agents but realized only by a few. I would now join the ranks of such notable agents as Clint Hill, Jerry Parr, Tim McCarthy, and Larry Buendorf, as well as the thousands of unknown agents who had since 1901 directly protected the president of the United States. After paying my dues and learning the basics of my profession for a decade, it was now my turn to help safeguard the leader of the free world from arm's length. I prayed I would be up to the task.

The New Guy, Again

In June 1993, on my first day as a PPD shift agent, I reported to W-16, the Secret Service command post in the West Wing. Briefing for the shift was at 0600, but I was always at least five minutes early. I found out that morning that everyone else was ten minutes early. I met my shift mates, and although I knew each of these agents, my shift leader introduced me and then we briefed for the day. I was happy with the lot I had drawn. These were good men, and two of them, Joe Clancy and Tony Meeks, were former CAT agents.

After briefing, we moved from our command post in the West Wing of the White House to the main mansion, where I had worked so many CAT midnight shifts over the past four years. We relieved the previous midnight shift, which was very glad to see us, and we moved to our posts.

Agent Jim Knodell, the senior agent on the shift, whose position was officially known as the shift "whip," walked me around to each post, explaining the responsibilities for each. Jim was a bit wary as to what my attitude was going to be because of my CAT experience. Although I had worked in the White House much longer than Jim and had filled in from time to time as a shift agent while in CAT, I did not know what the permanent shift responsibilities were, or the general shift routine. While an ace in CAT, I was essentially a shift "new guy," who happened to know how to move around the White House without getting lost.

After explaining the first post, Jim looked at me and asked, "Do you already know all of this?" I was not sure if he was busting my chops or really thought I might possibly already know the information he was relating to me. I said, "Jim, I don't know crap; please explain it all as if I had never set foot in the White House." After that, we got along well.

For a new agent on PPD, there were always some tough moments in learning the routine. Each day there seemed to be a never-ending list of new things to be learned, and most of them were unwritten. What information did exist in writing was provided on small flash cards, which reminded the agent of what their actions should be at each post. Also issued was a series of flash cards depicting the various formations used in walking with the president.

I had been on the shift about two weeks and was just learning enough about my duties to be a menace. One morning I was posted at the ground floor of the White House when the elevator light came on indicating "Eagle," the call sign for President Clinton, was on the way down in the elevator. The door to the elevator opened, and out came the president in a suit dressed for work. I quietly announced over my sleeve microphone, as was standard operating procedure (SOP), "Eagle moving to the Oval." Off we went, with me leading the POTUS to his office for another day of whatever presidents do. He did not need to be led, of course, but there always had to be an agent close by.

All was routine, and as we reached the Oval Office, I opened the colonnade door leading inside the room, with Eagle close behind. As we entered, I did a quick look-see to make sure all was in order and then exited through what I thought was the door leading to the hallway. It was not. I instead exited through the door leading into the private dining room of the Oval Office, which was located next to the door I was supposed to use.

With Bill Clinton in Georgetown, 1993. Bill Clinton loved large crowds, the larger the better. That is me on the far right wearing the game face. We had just emerged from the Sequoia restaurant in Georgetown on a Sunday morning into a large crowd and had been in one place far too long.

(Courtesy of the White House)

There was no one in the small dining room other than me standing there trying to decide what to do next. I should have taken another second or two to decide, because I made the wrong decision. I turned and reentered the Oval Office to find a surprised and somewhat annoyed-looking President Clinton. I tried to look as though this were all somehow planned, as I said, "Good morning, sir, all clear," and then exited through the correct door.

No one knew about this minor but embarrassing incident, and being new, I was certainly not going to inform on myself. Phil Hyde, my old team leader in CAT, was a big proponent of the old question: "If a tree falls in the forest and no one hears it, does it make a noise?" My going through the wrong door was a tree that had made no noise, and I was going to leave it that way.

Site Advances and Dealing with the Presidential Staff

Before the president leaves the White House for any reason, a security site advance is performed by the Secret Service at the location to be visited. It can be as simple as merely finding an arrival point for the motorcade, a bathroom, and the route to be walked, to the complexity of a two-week advance in a foreign country with multiple venues.

On each site advance, an agent is assigned a counterpart from the president's staff to work with. This staff person is responsible for what the president will do at the site, including activities and the sequence of events. The agent is then responsible for preparing a security plan around the president's itinerary. For an experienced agent, conducting a site advance is not particularly difficult, although it is time-consuming, detailed work. Any problems encountered in performing a site advance usually surface as a result of dealing with the president's staff.

On January 20, 1993, Bill Clinton moved into the White House, and along with him came a staff so different from that of George Herbert Walker Bush that they could have been from another planet. In direct contrast to the departing Republicans, most of whom were at least forty years of age, Clinton's staff had a mere handful of experienced, mature professionals. The remainder were an inordinate number of young people possessing no significant work experience. Many of these youngsters took time off, not from practicing law as some of the Bush staff had, but rather from law school. Some were younger than we agents by a decade or more, and almost all were initially arrogant and disrespectful of the Secret Service. In spite of their Ivy League educations, they just didn't seem to get it. Much of this attitude had to do with their youth and immaturity, as well as the disdain many seemed to hold for law enforcement in general.

To many of these young people, who were now in charge of planning the POTUS's schedule and who played a large part in the day-to-day running of the White House, this was nothing more than a grand cool adventure not taken seriously. It was also class warfare to a degree. Most of these youngsters were from wealthy families, and many viewed Secret Service agents as the hired help, although all agents possess at least a four-year degree and most on PPD enjoy six-figure incomes. On top of their seemingly willful ignorance, the junior staff could also be dangerous in an adolescent sort of way, as I was to discover.

Bill Clinton was visiting Russia in December 1993, and I was along for the trip. I had been preposted at an event, when a young staffer walked by and into the secure area about to be occupied by POTUS. This was not a concern as the staffer was known to me and was wearing the proper lapel pin identification that allowed total access to the POTUS area. The rub was that the Russian KGB agents assisting us did not understand our identification system and had no idea who this young man was who was now in a "do not admit area."

As the staffer was walking by, a KGB officer grabbed him by the arm to stop him. The staffer then jerked away from the Russian and continued on his way, as if he were dealing with a Wackenhut security officer in Toledo. As the KGB agent was about to do his worst, I put my hand on his shoulder (gently) and explained to him (he spoke English as most do) that the young man was one of the president's staff and that he had access to the area. I also asked that he not officially detain or confront the young man. He reluctantly agreed out of professional courtesy, an act that would cost me several rounds of vodka later while off duty with my Russian friend.

I later confronted the young staffer and in a tactful manner told him he had come very close to being taken into custody by the KGB for his immature, unprofessional behavior. He glared at me and then replied they couldn't do that to him because of his position on the presidential staff. I informed him he was in Russia, not America, and they could detain him if they wished since it was their country. He rolled his eyes and walked away.

While the young staffer offered no gratitude for my having plucked him from certain embarrassment and physical discomfort, I did not intervene in the situation for his sake. While it is every agent's job to protect the president from physical harm, it is also every agent's unofficial duty to protect the president from potential embarrassment when possible. For one of the president's staffers to be hauled away by the Russian authorities would have created embarrassment for the president. Even so, from that point on, I decided to never again intercede in any matter on behalf of this boy trying so desperately, yet unsuccessfully, to be accepted as a man in a world of which he had no understanding.

Another example of the maturity issues the Secret Service encountered with staff occurred in 1993 when I was sent to conduct advance for POTUS to Hilton Head, South Carolina. The site was a hotel ballroom where President Clinton would address a group of supporters from a stage. Secret Service doctrine is, and probably has been since the days of Teddy Roosevelt, that there will always be a means of evacuating POTUS from the rear of any stage he occupies. This is not negotiable in any way, and staff is well aware of the doctrine.

I was working well with a young female staff counterpart, and all was going according to plan until I left her unattended for a few minutes. When I returned, I found that she had blocked the rear of the stage, meaning our avenue of escape, with a movie-like set made of plywood. I had just explained to her not one hour earlier that we needed a clear exit to the rear of the stage, to which she had agreed. Perhaps she had not understood.

Just as I would explain to a child why he or she could not do a certain thing, I patiently explained to this twenty-five-year-old woman of the world that the set had to move and why. She stared at me with a look as if her father had just told her she couldn't go to the mall with her friends and get a tattoo or body piercing. She then proceeded to raise her voice and tell me that the set was going to remain where it was and she was not going to move it.

Secret Service agents have many items in their bag of tricks to get the job done, from words to guns, but the first and most effective is our intellect and tact. I once again tried to explain why the set had to go, or at least be modified to give us a way out using the rear of the stage. I used the word *modified*, meaning we could compromise, but we needed our way out. Once again, my patient attempts to reason were met with childlike emotion born of a past where no one in authority (probably beginning with her parents) had ever said no to her about anything. I was now dealing with a spoiled child, rather than a presidential staff person, and was very quickly losing what patience I had remaining. Finally I said, "Okay, I am going to go call the lead staff advance," who was her boss and was usually a little older than the site counterparts, almost thirty in some cases, and turn the matter over to him and the lead advance agent. They could battle it out.

As I walked away to make the call, I heard a person running up behind me. I turned to see my assertive counterpart in tears, begging me not to call her boss, the lead staff advance. This young woman had tried to intimidate and bully a thirty-nine-year-old security professional with her drama queen, emotional performance to get what she wanted. She had been testing me. It had probably worked most of her life with college professors, boys, and her parents. It did not work against the Secret Service, and I was unmoved by her tears. While I had first agreed to compromise, I was no longer in the mood and directed her, in a voice that could be heard for some distance, to get rid of the entire set—all of it, and right now. She did, and from that point on, we had no more issues.

She began to really work for me, doing whatever I directed, as I was no longer asking or suggesting but telling. I was also teaching her, and without her realizing it, she was learning. I suspected she was probably a nice person, but like most of the staff was young and immature and just needed some discipline, someone to figuratively kick her in the ass and say no occasionally. In this case, I was glad to be that person.

The visit went well, and upon departure of POTUS, the lead staffer congratulated her. Also upon POTUS's departure from our site, she hugged me and thanked me for all my help—and then asked if we could get together later on. I declined.

As fate would have it, I worked with this same woman again a few months later at a major site much more complicated than the one in Hilton Head. She was a totally different person. Much more mature, confident, and emotionally stable. This time we worked together, instead of me directing her or her trying to roll me. There were no problems during the advance or at the site. This staffer had begun to grow up and would be an asset to the president and the Service, but there were still too few like her.

In addition to their fundamental traits of rudeness and arrogance, the young staff's worst quality by far was total disorganization. They never had even a basic idea of POTUS's itinerary or sequence of events on the first several days of any advance. As a result of the staff's total inefficiency, we had a lot of time to roam around for the first few days of the advance. You always paid at the other end, however. About two days before POTUS's arrival, staff would come up with at least a half-assed itinerary, at which time we would put it all together. The result was that, although we had been in place for days, we now had only about forty-eight hours to do our advance.

This lack of purpose and organization by staff never seemed to change, although the Service and the staff eventually began to become used to each other and the relationships began to improve. There were fewer and fewer instances like the one in Hilton Head as the staff matured somewhat, in no small part to being around adult professionals in the Secret Service. They began to understand the reasons for the things we did and that they could not push agents around, as some probably had pushed around the hired help back at the old family estate. Some even began to develop a basic respect of authority and learned we were anything but the hired help and that a smart staffer would befriend an agent as much as possible whenever possible. They were learning lessons from the Service—one being that with great power comes great responsibility. This change also occurred as the result of the POTUS chief of staff working well with the SAIC of PPD and laying down the law among the junior staff, to stop being adolescent pains in the collective ass of the Service and start playing ball. If anything, junior staff were an intelligent lot, and most finally, although some reluctantly, got on board the team bus.

Foreign Counterparts

Advance counterparts on foreign trips could be anyone, including hastily vetted foreign nationals, but the advance was still run by the presidential staff. One such trip under President Clinton was to Aqaba, Jordan.

After arriving in country and checking into our hotel, we had a quick meeting with all the advance personnel and presidential staff to try and get an idea what President Clinton's itinerary would be. As usual, they did not know, and their ineptness in this case worked to my benefit. I had contracted a major case of food poisoning before leaving for this trip, and since the staff had no firm plan as yet, I got a little more desperately needed recovery time.

I was on this advance to do the transportation or motorcade portion of the trip. A large part of a transportation advance was the planning and running of routes the POTUS motorcade would be using. In the case of my motorcade advance in Aqaba, I was issued a little Jordanian who had been vetted by the American Embassy and bore an uncomfortable resemblance to Sirhan Sirhan, the man who killed Bobby Kennedy.

In the States, you usually did your advance with a local cop, who knew every street and every possible way to move from point A to point B. In this case, I had the young Jordanian, who always needed a shave and wore the same dirty T-shirt and jeans each day. He looked totally menacing, with dark, cruel eyes and a two-inch scar running down his right cheek. His demeanor suggested he was capable of cutting a man's throat and leaving him for the vultures should it become necessary. As with any foreign counterpart, the Secret Service had to assume people such as this were part of the host country's intelligence service, or worst case, a terrorist organization. I never trusted him entirely and was never comfortable with the amount of sensitive information he was acquiring.

After two full days of running all of the routes the president of the United States would actually be traveling the day of the visit, including routes to the hospital, police stations, and possible safe houses, my counterpart disappeared and was replaced with a Jordanian policeman. I asked our main Jordanian counterpart from the US Embassy what had happened to my little guy. I reminded him that this young man knew every inch of the POTUS motorcade routes, that it was too late to change them, and it was not a good idea for him to be at large.

The Jordanian diplomat, while smoking a cigarette that would make a Lucky Strike seem tame, informed me that his government had acquired some information that caused them to be concerned about my counterpart's allegiances. "But not to worry," he said, "he has been taken care of."

I was never sure what that meant exactly, but had a good idea of what it meant in that part of the world. I guess my counterpart was not vetted quite well enough.

On the day of the visit, as the presidential motorcade navigated its way through the narrow ancient streets of Aqaba, I could not help but constantly scan the open windows of the stucco homes. I half-expected to see one of my former counterpart's clones lean out of a window with a rocket-propelled grenade launcher (RPG for short) and put a rocket into the limo. I never saw my ex-counterpart again, however, and maybe no one else ever did either.

On to Israel

After the visit of POTUS to Jordan ended, our advance team was put on a bus at the Jordanian-Israeli border and driven all night to Jerusalem, where we would assist with the upcoming visit of POTUS. The good shepherd provided to watch over us by the Israeli government was a female Shin Bet, or perhaps Mossad, agent who gave her name as Rachel.

Rachel was quite different from most women I had ever personally met in the security field. Rachel had wild, wavy brown hair and a dark tan from the Israeli sun. She also had the most unusual scar running down her perfectly sculpted right bicep. It was jagged and uneven, not a surgical scar, but one caused by something from her unknown past that was hot and metallic. Although we were all armed, she was our protector as we rode in our bus on a brilliantly moonlit night through the Israeli countryside.

Being from a country that had fought for its survival on more than one occasion and was surrounded by countries that wished Israel exterminated, Israeli women were raised differently from American women—or women from almost anywhere. Israeli girls grew up learning how to use weapons, load ammunition magazines, and kill their country's enemies, while American girls grew up playing with dolls. Like all Israelis, each had to serve mandatory military service. Biologically, Israeli women and those from other countries were the same, but that is where the similarities ended.

At some point, we stopped at a small country store in the middle of nowhere. Rachel told us to get whatever we wanted, including beer. Back on the bus, almost everyone had a couple of beers since we had just completed one of the most stressful and dangerous advances of our careers in Jordan and needed to relax a little. The bus was not large, but there were only ten or so of us, so we each had our own row. It was a great time to reflect on the last mission and just enjoy traveling through the land where Jesus once walked.

In spite of suffering from terminal fatigue, our minds were still wound up from the last assignment and would not allow us to rest. No one talked and no one slept, but each merely sat alone with his or her own thoughts. The moonlight illuminating the ancient desolation was almost as bright as noon and was too beautiful to miss.

After several hours of driving and with the sun rising, we arrived at our hotel in Jerusalem. As we got off the bus and said good-bye to our lovely and most certainly lethal guide, Rachel shook hands with each of us with a soft but firm grip and then disappeared back to her life of serving Israel.

The Media

While I personally liked some members of the media, there existed during my PPD tenure an inherent adversarial relationship between the media and the Secret Service. Some members of the media were total professionals, who recognized and respected the rules set forth by the Secret Service, while others were totally rebellious and resentful of all Secret Service direction and authority.

This state of affairs existed due to polarization of purpose. While it is the job of the media to cover every public move of POTUS, it is the job of the Secret Service to insulate POTUS from anything that might potentially do harm and to keep the area in which POTUS operates as "clean" as possible, meaning clear of unnecessary bodies. I do not mean to imply that the media, including the White House press corps, is dangerous; they are not. Each has been thoroughly vetted and deemed safe to be around POTUS, although each must pass through metal detectors prior to being admitted to the White House grounds or aboard Air Force One. They are, however, perpetually in the way, too many in numbers, and a constant distraction to security by their presence alone.

All agents on PPD take turns escorting the media at presidential events. I never knew one who enjoyed the work, and in my case the sentiment was "extreme dislike." The main purpose of this assignment, known as "press agent," is to see to it that no assassin embeds himself in the press area, as John Hinckley did on March 30, 1981, when he shot President Reagan. The more practical everyday purpose is to ensure the press hurries along and does not delay the motorcade's timely departure.

In most cases during a motorcade departure, everyone, including the president, is in their vehicles ready to move out, while the hapless members of the media struggle to get into their vans with cameras, microphone booms, and all other manner of equipment going in all directions. Most tend to move without much purpose, and absent the constant prodding from an agent, they would take close to forever getting into their vans.

Each member of the media was always potentially difficult to work with. Many constantly pushed the envelope, and as with staff, agents did not become too friendly with any member of the media. To do so would create a familiarity that certain members of the press would exploit when it suited their purpose. One day they would be obedient and cooperative, and the next they would practically mutiny in order to get what they wanted. The leash they were kept on had to be held tightly and made very short.

The feeling of veiled animosity by Secret Service agents toward the media was returned with equal if not greater intensity by the press, concealed behind an expression of cold indifference. Each wished to roam about at will as the press agent herded them into areas that did not always meet with their approval. None enjoyed being told where they could and could not go, even though each knew it was a part of the game they had to play in order to keep their White House press credentials. This Holy Grail of press passes was issued by the Secret Service and was the hammer held by the Secret Service over the media. It could be used against out-of-control behavior, and the hammer did fall on occasion.

One day I witnessed an agent literally rip a press pass from the neck of a photographer who had pushed things too far on too many occasions. With the loss of the coveted pass, the photographer was now no different from the general public and was escorted from the area. Then, rather than ride in the press van, he was forced to take a series of taxicab rides from site to site, where he could observe only from the general public area.

The end of my association with the press occurred as the result of a physical confrontation I had with a print reporter while working a rope line with President Clinton. President Clinton was working the outdoor rope line on a trip that had a lot of stops. We had been on the road for several days, everyone was tired, and as usual the media and staff were testing everyone's patience with their "golly gee whiz" approach to things. As POTUS moved down this rope line, the limo paralleled along behind him in the event we had to move him quickly out of the area. My job was to walk alongside the limo manning, in this case, the left rear door, which was cracked open and ready for use if necessary.

All in the media are aware that no one is to get between POTUS and the door of the limo. On this day, however, a print reporter the size of Oliver Hardy continued to do so. It was a problem because if Rich, the detail leader, had to grab POTUS, turn him, and push him inside the limo, Ollie would be in the way. Twice I put my hand on Ollie's shoulder and firmly but politely asked him to move away from the door of the limo. Twice he ignored me. The third time I did not ask. I turned him around, and with all my strength and weight, which was about ninety pounds less than his, shoved him out of the way, at which time he went spinning in an uncontrolled manner toward the crowd.

**Keeping an eye on things with President Clinton
in the pressroom at the White House**

(Courtesy of the White House)

This rope line was so chaotic and was moving so fast no one seemed to notice the event, no one except one of Bill Clinton's senior staff. I say *senior* in the sense she was fairly high up in the staff chain of command although only in her thirties. She also did her share of getting in our way a great deal of the time, moving in our formations with a sense of irritating entitlement and no purpose.

After finishing the rope line, everyone boarded Air Force One for the trip to our next stop. After being airborne for about an hour, my shift leader informed me the senior staffer had complained to Rich Miller, the special agent in charge of PPD, about my tossing the reporter and wanted me removed from the detail. Rich reportedly calmed the staffer like a father would calm down a hormonally driven teenage daughter, and the incident died. The word from him to me through my shift leader was, however, to stop grabbing reporters. I never "grabbed" another reporter because I was never again assigned the job of press agent.

Nose of the Camel:
The Journalistic Media

Media association for the Secret Service came in many forms, from the dreaded job of press agent to allowing the journalistic media entry into what once was the very enigmatic and clandestine world of the United States Secret Service.

When I became a Secret Service agent in 1983, the Secret Service was a total mystery to most, and virtually no substantial amount of information about it existed outside the organization. The culture of the Secret Service during that era dictated that agents never publicly discussed weapons, numbers of agents, training, and tactics—and never under any circumstance did we publicly discuss the people we protected. To do so was to violate an unwritten code of silence observed by all agents of the Secret Service and risk being terminated from employment.

In those days, there was very little contact between the Secret Service and the journalistic media unless it was completely necessary. There seemed to be just enough contact to perpetuate one of the most powerful weapons in the Secret Service inventory: mystique. That is why most of the Secret Service was stunned when our training facility at the James J. Rowley Training Center in Beltsville, Maryland, was opened to Joan Lunden in the late 1990s for her *Behind Closed Doors* special. Enter the camel.

Prior to this TV special, agents would have been expected to hold out under torture to protect the information freely offered up to Joan. This TV special, authorized at the highest levels of the Secret Service, became the camel's nose under the tent flap in terms of allowing the media into our spaces, spaces where the entire camel now roams almost at will.

Joan's mission was to obtain as much information and gain as much access to the inner workings of the Secret Service as possible. She succeeded beyond her producer's wildest dreams, using all of her people skills both learned and innate to get that information. For those of us trained since being sworn in as agents to reveal almost nothing about our work, we could scarcely believe what we were witnessing.

There have been many other potentially harmful video presentations about the Secret Service, such as the one produced by the History Channel titled "The Secret Service," "Secret Service Files" by National Geographic, and the far-too-revealing "Secrets of the Secret Service" produced by the Discovery Channel. All of these video productions were in my opinion totally unnecessary, and their existence represents a danger to both agents and protectees alike. All terrorist attacks and assassinations begin with intelligence gathering, and there is no better source for information about the Secret Service and how it protects the president and others than these irresponsibly detailed documentaries, available to anyone with a personal computer.

Around the World with the President of the United States

Most think of traveling to locations such as Europe with the president while staying in the finest hotels as being glamorous and exciting. If you are an agent on PPD, however, traveling to exotic, faraway places means working long hours while experiencing jet lag and sleep deprivation and trying to keep your nutrition level to a point where you can function. A person's biorhythms become totally out of phase, and regularity habits kick in at the worst possible times.

On one such trip to Europe, I had been preposted by my shift leader in a large ballroom of a hotel where POTUS was to have a private, off-the-record meeting, meaning no press. It was a grand room and hotel, very old and ornate, with enormously high ceilings and priceless art work—all very European.

As I waited in the empty room for POTUS, my internal mechanisms began to rumble. This was trouble on a large scale. I knew I was entering into a situation in which I had to find a men's room, or even a ladies' room, or there would be an explosion too horrible to imagine. I hoped the feeling would pass and I could last until POTUS had his meeting, at which time I could be relieved—sorry for the pun—by another shift member while I found a privy. This situation was not going to end this way. I had to go, and within the next two minutes, and that was that.

For the first and only time in my Secret Service career, I abandoned my post and fled to the men's room across the hall from the room POTUS was due to arrive at literally any minute. The odds an assassin would appear in the next two minutes were probably zero, while the certainty that I had to find a men's room during that time was 100 percent.

I rushed into the ornate men's room and found a beautiful stall. Two minutes later, back in phase, I quickly reassembled equipment and myself and then ran to the door of the men's room to return to my post. I flung open the door to the men's room and literally ran into the president of the United States, William Jefferson Clinton, almost knocking him down. It seems his internal clock was still on Washington time, the same as mine. As I moved aside to allow him into the men's room, I quickly thought of a cover for action and blurted out in my most professional voice, "All clear, sir." He said, "Thanks, Dan," and entered to tend to his presidential business. My shift leader nodded to me, and we left the leader of the free world alone in his now-private bathroom.

As I moved back to my post across the hall, it occurred to me that my shift leader thought I was checking out the men's room for POTUS. It was too perfect, and I let him continue to think that forever. It could not have been any closer.

My son and I say hello to President Clinton in the Oval Office.

(Courtesy of the White House)

Not-So-Exotic Foreign Travel

I quickly learned that foreign trips on PPD were seldom exotic or exciting. On some trips, we could be in one of the most beautiful cities in the world and never really see the place, depending on what shift we were working. On one such trip to Budapest, I was working the 4:00 p.m. to midnight shift. It was already dark when we arrived, and we never left the hotel during my shift. We could have just as easily been in Cleveland and not known the difference.

After the anticipation and looking forward to a foreign trip to a nice part of the world, I frequently found that I was so tired after the flight and working twelve or more hours in some cases that all I wanted to do was sleep in the too-small beds in the too-small European hotel rooms. Once I had to store my bags in the hallway of the hotel, as there was not enough space in the Barbie doll-size room.

The saying in the Service was that no matter where you go, once you arrive, there you are. Generally speaking, that summed it up for me as far as foreign travel.

Scorpions and Syrians

All Secret Service agents constantly live with the reality that their lives are expendable and can be exchanged at any time for that of the president. That reality permanently resides in the back of an agent's mind, where it is not dwelled upon, yet is always there.

In every Secret Service agent's career, however, there are incidents that bring this reality home. One such incident occurred on a trip to Switzerland in 1993, where President Clinton was meeting with various heads of state, including the Syrian president and dictator Hafez al-Assad.

While the president of the United States traveled with just the number of agents needed to efficiently protect him, Assad, it seemed, traveled with every armed agent in Syria, most of whom were probably related to him in some way. Inevitably there were genetic problems associated with thousands of years of cousins marrying one another. I never knew where the less chromosomally lucky products of this civilization ended up, but those who could function usually worked in some capacity for the man in power.

Dictators such as Assad also traveled overseas with almost all of their military leaders. These men dressed in uniforms resembling something out of a cartoon, with more medals and awards than Audie Murphy although not as deserved. The idea was that if all his military leaders were with him, there would be no one to overthrow the government in his absence, although I saw this happen once while protecting the president of Sudan in 1983.

With the meeting between Clinton and Assad, the Secret Service was concerned about having so many armed Syrians in a relatively small room just feet from POTUS. Because of this concern, an agreement had been reached with the head of Syrian security that they would not be armed during the meeting. The thought behind this request was that, in addition to not trusting the Syrians in general, in any situation where gunfire might erupt, their doctrine was to empty magazines indiscriminately in all directions. With the Syrians unarmed, neither of these things would be an issue.

The problem was that with the Syrians, as with almost all people from the region, they would outwardly agree to almost anything and say, "No problem, no problem," when in fact they had no intention of following through with whatever it was they had no problem with. In most cases, they were not even listening to what was being proposed.

As a result of this known trait in their culture, my shift leader, Bob Byers, ordered me to prepost in the room with President Clinton and Assad, with the express purpose of neutralizing any threat to POTUS regardless of who posed the threat. Literally translated, that meant kill the Syrians if necessary. When I asked Bob for clarification of his instructions, he merely nodded. I suppose I should have been flattered to be chosen for such an assignment, but I realized that if I did have to shoot the Syrians, like them, I would be experiencing the last day of my life.

Prior to going into the room with Assad and President Clinton, I asked Bob why he had selected me for this unique assignment, rather than another member of the shift. He answered, "Because I know you will not hesitate to do what is necessary."

"Oh Bob, aren't you the flatterer?" I joked. Apparently he did not see the humor, as he wasn't smiling.

As directed, I preposted in the conference room, and as Assad entered, so did his security detail. As expected, they were not unarmed nor were they even trying to conceal the fact. As I slowly moved behind them into the best possible firing position, I noticed from the imprint of their too tightly fitting suit coats, these men were not only armed but carrying Scorpion machine pistols. I knew the Scorpion well and had fired them in CAT school during terrorist weapons familiarization training. As a result of this excellent training, I not only knew what type of weapon the Syrians were carrying, but what it was capable of. In a bind, I could also use one with good effect.

The Scorpion was a .32 caliber weapon with a ten- or twenty-round curved magazine that fired fully automatically, giving it little accuracy in any situation, especially in a packed room. It had a small folding stock that, when extended, came down over the forearm for added stability. The weapon itself was prone to malfunctioning and was really a piece of junk, but in such a venue, they would be deadly, and many would be shot, including perhaps the president of the United States. That, of course, could not be permitted.

As I stood behind my potential targets, I began running scenarios through my head playing the "what if" game. There really was not much "what if" in this case, other than if the Syrians drew their Scorpions, I would shoot each of them twice with my Sig Sauer pistol as rapidly as possible until the threat was neutralized, I had expended all ammunition, or I was out of the game.

As President Clinton and Assad sat at the front of the room side by side, and I stood behind the Syrian security agents, all of my senses were on full alert, peaking and then receding with every movement of my potential targets. If I had to respond to the Syrians, it would be the quintessential example of surgical shooting, taking out specific targets one by one in a room packed with innocents as well as the leader of the free world. In CAT, I had practiced this type of scenario many times and had fired thousands of rounds of ammunition preparing for such an occurrence.

I repositioned a bit in order to ensure POTUS and Assad would not be in my line of fire in the event I was forced to shoot and actually missed. As bad as a shoot-out in this small room would be, it would, of course, be catastrophic beyond imagination if a Secret Service bullet from my pistol struck either POTUS or Assad.

Due to the beyond-outstanding training received through the years from both the Marine Corps and the Secret Service, I felt confident. As in similar situations I had encountered through the years, I knew I had done all I could do to prepare for whatever might now occur, and a calm came over me as I stood ready to do what was necessary to protect the life of the president of the United States.

After what seemed like an eternity, the meeting finally ended uneventfully. I held my position until each of the Syrian security agents had exited the room and then returned to our command post, where I sat in the first chair I saw. Bob walked by and commended me on my choice of firing positions, and then commented with a smile, "Foreign trips are really fun, aren't they, Dan?" After responding what he could do with himself, which would have been anatomically impossible, I returned to my room to change shirts.

Air Force One

When it was time for PPD to travel, we traveled in a style that even the wealthiest could not buy a ticket for. We traveled on Air Force One, operated by the United States Air Force Special Air Missions (SAM) squadron.

The call sign "Air Force One" for presidential aircraft was first used by the Eisenhower administration in 1953, after an incident in which a commercial aircraft operating in the same airspace as Ike's also had the same call sign. Since that time, the call sign Air Force One has applied to any air force aircraft being flown in by POTUS. It makes no difference if the plane is one of the Boeing 747s built specifically for POTUS or a smaller Grumman Gulfstream business-type jet sometimes used by POTUS for short hops where using a full-size 747 is not practical. Technically the call sign could apply to a Cessna Birddog two-seat single engine aircraft if POTUS were aboard. If it is an air force plane and POTUS is aboard, it is Air Force One. If POTUS is not aboard, the airplane will have a normal air force call sign.

Presidents using airplanes for official travel is relatively new, with FDR being the first president to fly while in office. He really had no designated airplane in the beginning and flew a commercial Pan Am Clipper on one overseas flight. Two army air corps aircraft later were designated for him, but the Secret Service deemed one not usable due to its safety record and the other was only used on one occasion. President Truman had two different aircraft assigned to him during his presidency, but did not use them a great deal. Most notably, it was aboard one of these aircraft that he signed the bill that created the United States Air Force as a separate branch of the military in 1947.

While Eisenhower had flown on one or two occasions in jets as POTUS, JFK was the first president to actually use a jet for travel on a regular basis. It was symbolic in a sense. Presidents like FDR, Truman, and Ike were old and slow men, who traveled on slow propeller-driven aircraft. JFK was more like the Boeing 707. Both airplane and president were young, good-looking, and in a hurry to get places.

The first jet aircraft that would become the standard Air Force One (AF-1) was a Boeing 707, tail number 26000. In the beginning, this jet did not have the familiar blue, white, and gold paint scheme now identified with AF-1, nor did it have the large emblem of the president of the United States on the forward part of the fuselage. It was painted in orange and white colors with the letters identifying it as belonging to the United States Air Force. Not long after JFK entered office in 1961, tail number 26000 was given its new colors, which remain today the standard paint scheme for presidential aircraft.

The plane that took Kennedy on his most famous trips—including Berlin, where he made the famous "I am a Berliner" speech—was the 26000. It would also take him home for the last time on November 22, 1963, this time not riding in his usual area but in the aft end of the plane, confined to his coffin with Jackie sitting by his side.

In 1972, Richard Nixon took delivery of a new AF-1, another Boeing 707, with the tail number 27000. It then became the primary AF-1, and 26000 remained as the backup, but as operationally capable as 27000. Both of these aircraft would be used interchangeably as AF-1 until President George Herbert Walker Bush took delivery in 1990 of two new Boeing 747s, tail numbers 28000 and 29000. Both aircraft are identical, and both are still in service today.

After the new 747s arrived, Boeing 707 tail numbers 26000 and 27000 were relegated to backup duty but not retired completely from service until the mid 1990s. Both of these aircraft now reside in museums, with 26000 having served seven presidents and 27000 five.

A New Air Force One and the Disappearing Windshield

There was a world of difference between the older 707s and the new, much larger 747s. In addition to being significantly larger and more comfortable, the 747s' engines had a great deal more thrust than did the 707s. This initially caused some problems for CAT, which were dramatically brought to light quite unexpectedly one day.

One of CAT's main duties is protecting AF-1 on arrivals and departures. When the big jet is taxiing for takeoff and sitting at the end of a runway, or when it comes to a complete halt on landing rollout and no longer able to immediately lift back into the air, it becomes a gigantic fuel-bloated target of opportunity. It is the mission of CAT to defend AF-1 during these times of total vulnerability against attacks of all types, from organized with multiple attackers to someone running out of the woods to plant a charge on the landing gear. In order to provide this protection, the CAT truck must drive very close to AF-1 as it moves about on the ground, including giving chase down the runway during takeoff and landing. The noise in the CAT truck and buffeting from the engines' thrust is tremendous as CAT drives just yards behind the airplane. It was discovered quite by accident that this procedure had to be modified with the arrival of the larger 747s.

The first departure of 28000, one of the new 747s, occurred in 1990 from Andrews Air Force Base. From the CAT truck, the new airplane seemed twice as large as the old AF-1. As AF-1 taxied, an uneasy feeling began to spread through the vehicle when it was noted that the buffeting of the CAT truck from merely following the airplane during its taxi to the runway seemed as intense as the buffeting from the old Air Force One at full power.

On one of the early departures of 28000, with George Herbert Walker Bush on board, the CAT Suburban as usual upon takeoff fell in to provide

**From inside a CAT truck following Air Force One, tail number
27000, with President George Herbert Walker Bush inside.
Note the crack in the windshield from a previous encounter
with this jet. Although the engine thrust was less with this
airplane than the larger 747, it was still formidable. Damaged
windshields were not uncommon from following too closely.**

(Personal collection of Dan Emmett)

coverage behind AF-1—and it fell into a literal hurricane force of jet blast. The tremendous power from the four massive turbo fan engines, each providing 43,500 pounds of thrust, proceeded to blow the front windshield of the CAT truck into the laps of the driver and team leader.

Most sane, rational people, including Secret Service agents, would have called off the mission at that point, but CAT does not fall under this description. In best CAT tradition, which always includes finishing its mission, the truck continued to trail AF-1 down the runway, with the hot jet blast combined with dirt and debris ripping through the truck like a windstorm and the smell of burning jet fuel permeating every nostril in the vehicle. Due to the deafening roar of the engines, the sound of five CAT agents screaming and laughing in unison could not be heard, even by one another.

As the jet lifted off, the CAT truck turned off the runway onto the taxiway for its trip back to the ramp with no front windshield. A debriefing was later held, at which time it was decided CAT airport tactics were to be modified. CAT would continue to provide chase for AF-1 but from a greater distance.

Marine One

As with Air Force One, the president must be on board a marine helicopter in order for the call sign to be Marine One. Otherwise, the helicopter retains a standard Marine Corps identification. The army and Marine Corps once shared the duties of flying the presidential helicopter, but in 1976, the marines took over exclusively in this area. Much old footage exists of Ike and JFK flying in Sikorsky H 34 helicopters with ARMY on the fuselage. In such cases, the call sign of the helicopter would have been Army One.

The Marine Corps squadron tasked with the honor of flying the president is HMX-1, based out of Marine Corps Air Station Quantico, Virginia. "H" stands for helicopter, "M" for marine, and "X" for experimental, denoting the squadron's original mission of testing new, experimental helicopters. While the squadron flies many different types of helicopters, it transports POTUS primarily in Sikorsky VH-3 "Sea Kings," as seen below.

Marine One departs the White House.

(Courtesy of the White House)

Flying Onboard Air Force One

In an agent's career, there are certain things that will always stand out and be remembered forever. One of the most memorable events in my career was the privilege of flying on Air Force One, especially for the first time.

Flying on AF-1 to me was always special, and for many reasons. Nothing symbolizes the power and prestige of the presidency and the United States more than this magnificent aircraft. It is also special because only a very small percentage of Secret Service agents will ever fly on AF-1. For a Secret Service agent to fly in this airplane, one had to be assigned to PPD, and our numbers were relatively few compared to that of total agents in the Secret Service.

My first flight on AF-1 occurred in the summer of 1993, at night. My shift and I began this adventure by driving from the White House to an off-site landing zone, where boarded our own HMX-1 helicopter for the trip to Andrews, where we would board AF-1.

We arrived at the landing zone and proceeded into the HMX-1 complex through a gate manned by a heavily armed marine. After checking all of our credentials, the marine waved us through the gate; we found a parking slot and then got out and entered the ops building. Our helicopter arrived shortly thereafter and settled into its landing zone, whereupon the pilot disengaged the rotors and let them come to a stop, but with the engine still running at idle, creating a low whining noise. When cleared by the marine in HMX-1 operations, we proceeded out of the building to board the green Sikorsky VH-3 with the white top and "United States of America" painted on the aft end of the fuselage.

As I approached the waiting helicopter with my shift, I was immediately impressed by the beauty and sound of this unique flying machine, including the wonderful smell of burning jet fuel, the noise of the engine, and the perfect marine sergeant at the bottom of the aircraft's steps.

As we boarded the helicopter, the marine sergeant in full dress blues who stood by the forward steps saluted as we all got on board. The salute was not to honor us as anything more than what we were, but rather a standard courtesy rendered by the marine aircrew for anyone who boarded their helicopter. As a former marine officer, I instinctively returned the squared-away sergeant's salute, although it was not part of protocol. Protocol or not, as a former marine officer, it was a habit I would never break.

No sooner were we in our seats than the recruiting poster-perfect sergeant climbed in and pulled the entry hatch shut, fastening the latch behind him. He then leaned into the cockpit, where he talked briefly with the pilots before strapping into his seat. The pilots engaged the rotors and began to increase power until the rotors were spinning above us with a comforting but muffled sound and the bird began to vibrate from the torque of the turning rotor shaft. The crew quickly completed their pre-takeoff checklist, and very suddenly the helicopter began to rise as the pilot applied power and pulled up on the collective stick.

Up we went into the purple night sky and began to circle slowly over Washington. We flew in a type of holding pattern as we waited for Marine One bearing POTUS to lift off from the White House, at which time we would fly together in formation to Andrews.

The sun had just set on this clear night, and Washington was brilliantly illuminated, with the monuments standing out like giant white carvings placed on a toy landscape. The noise of the VH-3's engine was muffled by the sound insulation, and thus it was amazingly quiet, so quiet in fact that you could actually carry on a conversation with the person next to you without yelling. The last marine helicopter I had flown on was in 1981. It was another product of Sikorsky, a CH-53 Sea Stallion that was so loud one could not talk over the noise. It also had a noticeable puddle of some type of fluid in the floorboard. The 53 was designed to carry marines and their equipment into battle or anywhere else they needed to go. They did not need to be clean, quiet, and pretty. The presidential VH-3s, however, were designed to carry POTUS and his entourage in total comfort and style.

After circling for about twenty minutes and watching the same sights pass underneath several times, I could feel we were changing heading. As I looked out my window, I could see the red and green lights of Marine One rising up to meet us from the direction of the White House. As it neared, I could clearly see the shape and outline of the president's helicopter as it took the lead; we flew along in a trail position. Along the way, we changed the lead position more than once for security purposes.

As we began our approach into the Andrews Air Force Base area, I could feel the change in pitch of the rotors as well as the power setting. We came in from the west and descended lower and lower until we were in a hover just feet above the concrete, and then the marine aviator flying our helicopter touched down with scarcely any notice. We taxied to our position, where the pilot parked the aircraft and shut down the engines. The recruiting poster sergeant unlatched the door and lowered it. He then turned and nodded to us, indicating we were free to leave the helicopter and go to where we would begin the next part of our adventure. We quickly disembarked the Sikorsky, and as we left, the pilots, still seated, turned to their left and right to wave good-bye to us.

In about five minutes, Marine One was hovering over the tarmac and landed just as gently as had our helicopter. The pilot disengaged the rotors and shut down the engines. The front door opened and dropped into position, at which time another perfect marine sergeant, in the same perfect dress blues as ours, walked down the steps and to the rear of Marine One. There he unfastened and lowered an identical set of stairs for the passengers in the rear of the helicopter to descend.

Down the rear stairs descended the Secret Service detail leader and another agent, who picked up their designated places on the tarmac. Next exited President Clinton, who walked down the front steps, where a marine saluted him. He then began the short walk from Marine One to the front stairs of Air Force One. He ascended the front stairs and paused at the top, where he waved and then disappeared inside.

At this point, we were free to board Air Force One, but not immediately. The agents always board the rear steps of the aircraft. At the bottom of the stairs standing on the tarmac is an air force sergeant with a list of all who are supposed to be flying on AF-1 that day. After you provide your name to the air force sergeant, he checks you off the list, and then you literally run up the stairs and on to the plane as it is only moments from moving out.

I stepped up to the sergeant, gave him my name, which he checked off, and up the stairs I went to the Secret Service compartment of the airplane

toward the rear of the plane. This was just in front of the compartment
used by the White House traveling press corps. I then prepared for my first
flight aboard Air Force One.

I took my coat off and hung it in a closet next to our own lavatory,
while keeping my gun and radio on. Even though we were on AF-1, we
were still working and expected to respond if needed to any crisis. POTUS
was up front in his area, being watched over by the detail leader, where
there are two seats designated for the Secret Service.

I sat down in an oversize first-class type of seat, which was standard
throughout the plane, with my shift mates similarly seated. The next
thing I noticed was our shift leader closing the door that separated our
compartment from that of the media. Our compartment had its own
movie screen, and we began looking at the movie choices for the flight.
All we had to do was select the one we wanted and push the button that
corresponded to that movie, and it would run automatically.

As I settled in, an air force enlisted person came by and cheerfully
offered sodas, coffee, or snacks. This, I happily realized, was par for the
course on AF-1. If it were mealtime, they would bring delicious sandwiches,
which always tasted better than anything from the best restaurants. This
great service provided by the air force was especially welcome after a long
day out with POTUS in large crowds, some of which had not been through
metal detectors. We would frequently arrive back at the plane exhausted
and a bit stressed from a long day of keeping the leader of the free world
alive. No sooner would we take off our coats than the air force steward
would be there with drinks, snacks, lunch, or dinner.

As I sat watching the movie selected by our shift leader and drinking
a Coke, the engines of the airplane began to spool up, and we began to
move. AF-1 taxied for what seemed a long time as it moved down the
taxiway toward the end of the runway. I looked out my window and saw
CAT move back and into its trail position to protect us from unwanted
attention while on the ground; I hoped they would stay back far enough
not to lose another windshield.

We moved directly onto the runway after being cleared for immediate
takeoff by the tower and began the takeoff roll. The engines came up to

full power, and their combined thrust pushed us back in our seats as we continued to accelerate down the runway. We were picking up speed very quickly but still lumbering down the runway as only this gigantic plane could lumber. Upon reaching the required speed, the pilot rotated the nose, and up we went into the night sky. Sitting toward the rear of the plane, it seemed as if we were going straight up as we heard the motors that powered the flaps and landing gear push them into the up position and then heard the solid "bump" of the landing gear doors closing. We were in the air, and I was now flying for the first time on Air Force One.

As comfortable as it was to fly on Air Force One, an agent was still technically working and was expected to be able to respond to an emergency if necessary. Also, Service protocol dictated that an agent should remain as alert and professional on Air Force One as in the White House. Consequently one could never really relax during these flights. On this flight, as would be the case on many others, as we watched our movie (which was allowed), I looked up to notice President Clinton standing in our section preparing to move into the next compartment and conduct an impromptu media session. Our shift leader opened the door separating us from the media, and the president went in, with the shift leader trailing. After the president answered a few questions from the White House traveling press, he moved back through our compartment, where he stopped briefly to offer some friendly words to our shift before returning to his compartment.

After awhile, the sound of the engines lessened, and the plane's nose began to drop. This was the obvious sign that we had begun our descent, and it was our signal to start getting ready. For security reasons, such as avoiding shoulder-fired heat-seeking missiles, AF-1 always came in at a fairly steep rate of descent, and the pilot got the plane on the ground as soon as possible. On this, my first flight in AF-1, I was still putting on my jacket when the main landing gear hit the runway. It was dark and I was a bit startled when we landed, not realizing how close we were to the ground.

The entire shift was up and walking around while the plane was braking and the pilot going to reverse thrusters. We were bouncing and staggering around as if we were riding a rough section of train track. The plane had no sooner braked to a halt than our rear door was opened by a crewmember and we ran down the stairs and out into the waiting night to protect the president of the United States. On this day, I had completed my first ride on an HMX-1 helicopter and Air Force One as a full-fledged member of the Presidential Protective Division.

Reverent Russians and Flying in the Backup

On a trip to Russia in 1993, my shift had completed its assignment for the trip, and rather than fly home commercial, we were lucky enough to be manifested on the backup plane. We were all dead-tired after a week of protecting President Clinton in the streets of Moscow, Kiev, and other cities around the old Soviet Union, where he would frequently stop the motorcade, get out, and move among the Russians. The people were dumbfounded that an American president would be so open to them, as were we agents. We did, however, have the distinct advantage of being in a country not long out of the grips of Communism, where people automatically and without question moved when a security official said to move.

We were driving through the streets of Moscow on the way to the airport, where our shift would relinquish its responsibilities to another shift, which would fly home on AF-1 with POTUS. We were feeling pretty good, although tired, as we were heading for the homestretch on this marathon trip of sleep deprivation, when Clinton ordered the driver of his limo to stop. I was in the follow-up vehicle with the rest of my shift when we saw the limo's brake lights illuminate and the giant car begin to slow. We then heard the voice of the detail leader call out, "Halfback from Stagecoach, Eagle wants to work the crowd," Eagle being President Clinton.

As the cars halted, the detail leader emerged from the right front seat of the limo as we on the shift moved quickly to our positions. The detail leader opened the right rear door, from which President Clinton emerged, and we went into our designated formation, where we worked the president very closely.

Air Force One above Mt. Rushmore

(Courtesy of the White House)

The weather that day was a damp, bone-chilling cold one can only find in Russia. As we moved toward the large crowd in the street now surrounding the motorcade, we expected to be mobbed. Rather than the people swarming us, however, everyone who had been moving on the busy streets of Moscow began to quietly move to the sidewalks and stand motionless and mute. What the hell?

The hell was that as soon as we had stopped, the largest, meanest-looking men I had ever seen anywhere, many of whom looked like Dolph Lundgren from *Rocky IV,* materialized looking stereotypically Russian in great coats, traditional big furry Russian hats, and large boots. They were also armed with SKS carbines and AK-47 rifles. These men looked like pure evil, with cadaver-pale skin, blank expressionless faces, and very cruel eyes. They scarcely had to speak or give commands in order to control the crowd.

Clinton shook hands with the people who stood reverently on the sidewalk. We knew, however, that the only thing standing between a mob scene and us were these Russian policemen, whom the masses were obviously terrified of.

Clinton finally seemed to grow tired of shaking hands with the Russian citizenry—or perhaps he realized Russians couldn't vote in American presidential elections—and he returned to his limo. As we began moving back to the follow-up vehicle, I walked past one of our evil protectors who had the face not of Dolph Lundgren but more like Lurch from the *Addams Family.* He halfway extended his large gloved hand out to shake mine, which I did without hesitation.

We arrived back at the airport and pulled up next to Air Force One, where our relief shift met us and immediately took over. We gratefully acknowledged the passing of the human baton known as POTUS and started heading over to the backup plane parked about fifty yards away. Upon giving our names to the air force sergeant at the bottom of the stairs, we staggered on board, numb from the cold and bone-tired. Upon collapsing in our seats, we were greeted by the always-cheerful air force steward, who instead of offering the usual Cokes, offered beer. Since we were now off shift and POTUS was not onboard this aircraft, we were free to relax as if we were flying first class on British Airways. We each drank a few beers and watched a movie with no fear of POTUS appearing and then slept most of the way back to Washington.

Flying the President's Cars

When the POTUS travels out of Washington onboard Air Force One, his limousines travel via air force transport. Although both aircraft are operated by the United States Air Force, there is a world of difference in the ride.

During the 1980s and '90s, Lockheed C-5 Galaxies and C-141 Starlifters were used to fly the presidential cars. Both of these giants were designed to move entire military units and all of their equipment anywhere in the world in a short amount of time. They were also perfect for moving presidential limos and support vehicles, along with legions of personnel, anywhere in the world. The 141s carried the basic package of spare limo, limo, and follow-up. The C-5s carried six to eight vehicles and were used more on overseas flights.

The C-5, in addition to carrying major cargo, can also carry passengers, with an upstairs deck containing ninety-plus airline-type seats. In addition to delivering the POTUS vehicles to where they needed to go, it was also the most economical way to transport the many agents needed to stand post on the middle perimeter of a POTUS event. For the cars, it was a great way to go; for an agent flying the C-5 or C-141, it was always misery, which one learned through experience how to adapt to.

Old and worn-out, first by constant use in the Vietnam War, then by constant use in Desert Storm, the 141s should have been retired to the desert storage area in Arizona years before, but the C-17, which was to replace the C-141, had yet to go operational in sufficient numbers to help our mission. As a result, the tired C-141 by necessity flew onward in support of the president.

The 141s were noisy and slow, and the temperature inside was impossible to control. From your feet to your knees, you were numb with cold. From your knees on up, you were burning alive. Earplugs were necessary to avoid permanent hearing loss, although I did not escape that damage due to these and other loud noises, much to the annoyance of my wife, who has to yell at me in a noisy setting to be understood.

Another downside to the 141s was that they always broke, thankfully never in the air, but usually when you really needed to go somewhere in a hurry. It was more common than not for a replacement bird to be flown in from the closest base and the cars and people moved from the broken-down plane to the one that could still fly.

On one memorable landing, we hit the runway hard, very hard. The three armored vehicles were straining at their chains, and everyone was thinking about what would happen if one broke loose. Even though we had no window to look out of, it was obvious we were going faster than the normal landing speed. The brakes were squealing, and we could smell them burning. Thankfully, we finally came to a stop, and the pilot turned off the runway onto the taxiway.

I spoke to the aircraft commander after we shut down, as the rear end of the plane was opened to disgorge the cars. He was happy to talk about what had happened, because he was obviously proud of his flying skills in having kept us from crashing. It seems we almost ran off the end of a runway while landing because the power bus that operated the flaps failed. With no flaps to help slow our airspeed during final approach, we landed at too high a speed. The talented young captain managed to get the mammoth airplane stopped just before going into the weeds.

There were other close calls, as well, but no actual crashes of the 141 with Secret Service personnel or cars onboard. In spite of its mechanical glitches due to old age, only twenty-two of 285 were lost due to accidents during its entire service life, an incredible safety record for hours flown.

The routine to get the cars on the planes and into the air was standard. The day of the lift, several Secret Service personnel from PPD Transportation Section would meet at the main Secret Service vehicle garage, where all protection vehicles are stored and maintained. The current state-of-the-art facility's location is classified, and I will not reveal its whereabouts, although Joan Lunden and her film crew have been there.

All three vehicles—limousine, spare limousine, and follow-up—would depart the garage together en route to Andrews Air Force Base. Before leaving the garage, the checklist of items to be carried in each vehicle was verified, such as the proper number of Heckler and Koch MP-5 submachine guns, radios, first aid kits, and so forth. After confirming that all equipment was in the vehicles, the package departed the garage and made its way to Andrews, where the cars were driven onto the plane.

The Air Force Load Master of the crew always did a perfect job of chaining the cars securely down, but it was the responsibility of the agent designated to drive the limo to ensure it was done correctly. It always was, and the checking of tie-downs by the agent was always a mere formality. The proper securing of the cars was absolutely critical. Should one come loose at anytime in the flight, especially during takeoff or landing, the monsters would crush people and cause damage, possibly including loss of the aircraft.

Fuel could not exceed one-half tank in the cars to be flown because of the sloshing about of the fuel during times of turbulence and the expansion of air inside the fuel tanks at altitude would cause spillage. Occasionally it did not work out that the level of fuel was correct, and the smell of gasoline fumes from the cars could cause nausea for anyone sitting too near.

When the Secret Service was aboard their airplanes, the air force always went the extra mile to be as accommodating as possible. To ride in a C-141 Starlifter or even the newer C5 Galaxy was uncomfortable at best for long overseas flights lasting ten or more hours, and we always appreciated the courtesy and professionalism of the Military Airlift Command (MAC).

After takeoff, we would walk around the airplane and visit with each other, while those who discreetly brought their own beverages onboard would indulge in quiet moderation to help the sleep process. After tiring of yelling over the noise of the engines, we would return to our seats, which were either airline-type seating that could be put in or taken out on pallets depending on the mission, or—God forbid—the dreaded nylon web sling seats that folded down from the longitudinal axis of the airplane. Eventually everyone would try and sleep for a while until arriving at the next location.

Sleep did not come easily going to our destinations, but coming back to the United States, everyone was always exhausted and went out immediately. Going back to my marine days, I could always sleep anywhere, either sitting up or lying down. One did not lie down to sleep on the floor of a car plane, however—it could be fatal.

These airplanes were very cold close to the floor. This was due to having virtually no insulation between the thin skin of the airplane and the subzero outside air temperature. Returning from one overseas trip, an agent lay down in the aisle to get some sleep. He did sleep, almost forever. While sleeping on the freezer-temperature floor, his body lost a great deal of heat, and he went into hypothermia. When he was discovered shivering uncontrollably and the situation became clear, the airplane had to land as soon as possible in order to get the agent to a hospital. He survived his ordeal, but not by much. Had the air force not done such a great job in getting the plane to an alternate landing field where the agent could receive immediate attention, he would not have survived.

A Flying Treasure Ship

There were two major advantages to flying the car plane on overseas trips. One was that you did not have to bother with the always-annoying process of clearing foreign customs and immigration, as the American Embassy handled that formality. The other was that it provided the perfect means of getting all of your shopping items, no matter how bulky, back to the United States. It was only a matter of getting your purchases back to the plane, and the air force would load it all for you as long as it was not alive, illegal to have, or potentially harmful to the plane, crew, and passengers.

Many places we visited around the world had excellent shopping at great prices. In places such as Korea, the Philippines, and Europe, there were almost always great deals on almost any item you could think of. In some countries, you could literally buy anything from machine guns to people. We, of course, stuck to things that would be legal to have in the United States, and to my knowledge no one ever brought anything home that was illegal. We were, after all, federal law enforcement officers who valued our great jobs. No one was going to risk losing that job over trying to smuggle contraband back home.

On one trip, an agent brought home an entire brass bed. Another lugged home enough wine to keep him from going to the package store for quite some time. Most of us settled for smaller things we could carry on the plane or store in one of the cars transported on the plane. In CAT, we usually took our own Suburban on overseas trips. On the trip home, the vehicle would be loaded up with all types of great merchandise acquired while on the trip.

CAT always became instantly popular on such trips, as everyone wanted to use our truck for storage of their purchases. We were all in this together, so we usually allowed other agents use of the truck, unless by team vote it was decided that for any number of reasons the person making the request should not be allowed to use the CAT truck. These reasons usually included, first and foremost, whether the person was a CAT hater or CAT supporter. In a case where the requestor was voted to be a CAT hater, the agent would be told there was no room for his purchases, and once such a decision had been made, there was no possibility of reversing it other than by unanimous team vote.

On one such occasion after we rendered our opinion, the rebuffed agent became indignant, stating the truck did not belong to us but the government, and he could store his things in it if he wanted. We, in turn, reminded this young GS-7, whose ink on his graduation diploma from agent school was not yet dry, that while the truck may technically belong to the government, it was assigned to CAT, thus making it ours, and if he tried to put his items there, we would promptly damage his items as well as him. He stormed away mumbling something about CAT guys and found storage for his items elsewhere.

Gaudy Treasures

Almost every agent who has ever been on a foreign trip has in his or her home some hideous item purchased overseas and brought home on the car plane. A lot of these items looked great and had terrific novelty at the time of purchase. Upon getting them out of the country from which they were purchased and back home, many such items lost their shine almost immediately.

Once, in Turkey, I bought what I thought was a great-looking brass vase I thought my wife would love. After getting it home, I proudly presented it to her as a sign that although I had been halfway around the world, I was thinking of her. She took one look at the thing, and it was immediately relegated to the garage until picked up by Goodwill.

On the same trip, I purchased a giant water pipe. The enormous thing sat on the floor in our downstairs television room for about one day. In very short order, it joined the brass vase in the garage, along with an assortment of other tacky items, such as swords from Saudi Arabia just recently discovered in our last move. Two men who recently did some work on our home are now the proud owners of these implements of destruction. The lethal-looking items may now adorn their respective residences, or lie under a bed to be used in the event of a home invasion. (Perfect, if a roving band of killer nomads break down the door demanding your women.) They could also quite possibly be in a garage awaiting the Goodwill truck.

Still, upon arrival back at Andrews Air Force Base in Maryland, we had to clear US Customs inspections and declare our items. This was done on the airplane quickly with as little fuss as possible due to our being fellow Treasury agents and our usual poor condition of health that resulted from the mission we had just completed.

Running with the President

While on PPD, one of the most important missions I helped perform was running alongside President Clinton. My job was not to be his running buddy, but to keep him from getting killed while running through Washington, DC, either by assassins or traffic.

Prior to Bill Clinton's presidency, no president in the history of the United States had engaged in any serious physical fitness activities. President Reagan took naps and rode horses for relaxation, and President George H. W. Bush played tennis and golf, and ran on very rare occasions, usually only at Kennebunkport, Maine, the family compound.

Most pre-Clinton PPD agents were generally healthy and their weight was in proportion to their height, but most did not work out to any great extent. Up until Clinton and the relatively new threat of terrorist attack, PPD had been largely a gentleman's assignment, where looking the part combined with proper instincts and reactions was almost all that was needed. The responsibilities of the PPD agent, which had always included being perfectly groomed, were about to expand to also being physically fit. Agents would now be required to run as far as three miles with the president, wearing a gun and radio, and in the beginning many were not up to it.

Bill Clinton became a candidate for president of the United States in 1992 and had not spent a great deal of his life in pursuit of fitness. During the '92 campaign, he began to run as a form of exercise and to meet voters. One way to do this as a candidate was to run in public places, where the people were. He would sometimes complete his run at a local McDonald's to move among the voters and engage in nutrition that negated many of the benefits he had just received from the run. His habit of running began to present over time a huge security challenge to the Secret Service.

In order to properly protect candidate Clinton during these public runs, at least one or two agents had to run alongside, close enough to deal with any threat that might present itself. And they had to run with a pistol as well as a radio. In the beginning, this was not too difficult a challenge. Clinton was still a candidate, and only a couple of agents were needed to run, as his detail was much smaller than that of a sitting president. These two agents did not need to be in any high degree of fitness because Clinton did not run very far or fast.

In the beginning, the whole running thing with Clinton was as much about media coverage as fitness. The important thing was to get out and be seen, to appear fit, healthy, and energetic, all desirable traits in a president. As time progressed, he lost weight and actually began to get into a rudimentary level of fitness. He also began running farther and faster, and the Service was getting worried. Pretty soon there would exist the need for agents who were actually in good physical condition, not just barely getting through the run.

On January 20, 1993, William Jefferson Clinton, former governor of Arkansas and neo but now regular jogger, was sworn in as the forty-second president of the United States. An uneasy feeling began to spread among the aerobically unfit agents of PPD.

Secret Service management, as well as many on PPD, hoped that after inauguration, Clinton would knock off the running. To the contrary, however, and much to the anguish of those responsible for his direct safety, not only did Clinton not stop his running habit, he increased it. And to double the horror, he insisted on conducting his running not within the safe confines of the White House grounds, but in broad daylight on the streets of Washington, DC. The issue had now become very serious. The president was regularly running the mean and always potentially dangerous streets of Washington during morning rush hour in front of God and everyone, and there were not enough agents fit enough to handle the challenge.

One attempt to solve the problem resulted in a running track being constructed around the perimeter of the lower roadway on the south grounds of the White House. It was exactly one-quarter mile around, and it was hoped that would satisfy the president. If he ran there, only one or two agents would actually be required to run with him. It would largely be a matter of posting a few agents in strategic locations—but Clinton hated the track and did not use it.

While the running track idea was a failure, the new approach was to try and steer Clinton toward safer running venues, such as nearby military bases. Half of Clinton's purpose in running, however, was to be out among the people and to escape the confines of the White House, which Harry Truman once referred to as a prison. While going to places like Fort McNair, a few miles from the White House, made sense and actually provided as good as or better a place for him to run, he would have none of it. He wanted to run the streets and monuments of Washington, DC, just like anyone else.

Each shift had at least one or two agents who could run three miles at Clinton's usual nine-minute-per-mile pace. The problem was that one or two were not enough. At a minimum, four shift agents and a supervisor were needed, and each had to not merely possess the endurance to finish the run, but also enough reserve energy for responding to an emergency

President Clinton and I leaving the White House for a run through downtown Washington, DC, where anyone could be waiting with a gun

(Courtesy of the White House)

during or at the end of the run. Enter the Counter Assault Team (CAT) to the rescue.

While many supervisors on PPD had no clue how to make the best use of CAT, there was one very visible advantage to having these buffed weapons experts now a part of PPD: each could run forever while burdened with weapons and radios. The decision was made that every morning until whenever there were enough shift agents who could run three miles, CAT would provide runners to augment the shift. Due to their superior fitness level, as well as outstanding tactical skills, CAT literally saved PPD from disaster concerning the running issue during the early years of Bill Clinton's administration.

CAT had been a part of PPD for about a year at this point and was happy to help out, although this new CAT responsibility did not go well with some of the coat-and-tie boys that could not handle the running themselves. To ask for CAT assistance was demeaning to some, but the public image the Service had enjoyed for decades of being mysterious supermen who protected the president was suffering. Something had to be done.

One day the SAIC of PPD called a meeting with all available PPD agents in an auditorium of the Old Executive Office Building across from the White House. The purpose of the meeting was to lay down the law to his agents that this president ran almost every morning, that it was the responsibility of agents to run with him, and that everyone was going to be required to help out by taking their turn on the runs.

Without any training or preparation, some otherwise very good agents, who looked as out of place in shorts and running shoes as they were out of shape, began attempting to comply with the SAIC's orders.

CAT agents usually ran in the front of the formation because, by training, they possessed the highest degree of tactical expertise and situational awareness. In short, they could run while simultaneously surveying the area for possible ambush sites, not merely keep up on the runs.

After a few incidents of supervisors having problems keeping the pace, CAT began more and more to be assigned trail as well as point, requiring even more CAT agents to be pulled from the schedule to run. The reason more CAT agents were needed was that if the senior agent running next to POTUS dropped too far behind to be of any use, he would turn and motion a CAT agent to move up and take over his position of running next to the president. This required an agent to be able to sprint and quickly close the distance between his rear position and where POTUS now ran.

There was no such thing as an uneventful run with Bill Clinton. On one outing, we had begun the run at the reflecting pool in front of the Lincoln Memorial, dismounting the motorcade on Seventeenth Street in the middle of morning rush hour. This was a particularly memorable run for several reasons. The first thing that happened, even before the run began, was that a motorist driving south on Seventeenth Street looked to his right, where he was amazed to see the president of the United States in running apparel. Astounded, the motorist stared at the president until he rear-ended the car in front of him. Since we always traveled with a District of Columbia Metro Police-marked unit, the police were automatically already on the scene. After staring at the accident like a bewildered tourist, Clinton began his run.

Our route took us around the reflecting pool at the Lincoln Memorial, where Dr. Martin Luther King Jr. made his "I Have a Dream" speech in 1963. The run was going as it normally did, with Clinton plodding along at his usual nine- to ten-minute-per-mile pace. After one lap around the pool, Clinton, to the surprise and horror of all, crossed Seventeenth Street without the benefit of the crosswalk and ran toward the Washington Monument. This was not his usual routine of two or three times around the reflecting pool and then home.

The change of plan psyched out the supervisor running with him; thinking the run was done, he now began to fall back. Clinton, after crossing Seventeenth Street, continued to run up the gradual but increasingly steep incline toward the Washington Monument and multitudes of tourists. At least, he had not been run over crossing the street.

I was running trail and watched as the supervisor began to fall back, while the POTUS continued to open the distance between him and us. When it became apparent the supervisor was not going to make it, he looked back and signaled for me to take the off-shoulder position with

Clinton. This required me to sprint uphill a good seventy-five yards to close the distance between my position and POTUS, who was now totally without agent coverage and seemingly unconcerned about it. I ran past the supervisor and continued sprinting with a reserve energy born of adrenaline, as much as aerobic fitness, trying to close the distance before POTUS disappeared over the top of the hill and into the unknown.

Just as POTUS reached the crest of the hill where the monument sits, I caught up with him, and we came face-to-face with about thirty unbelieving tourists standing at the base of the monument. Each began scrambling for what I hoped were cameras as I moved between them and POTUS while placing my right hand inside my running jacket around the grip of my pistol. As we descended the hill, with me now running while looking over my shoulder to keep an eye on the tourists at the monument, there was no other agent in sight. Everyone was still on the reverse slope, trying to get up the hill.

Not long after topping the hill, President Clinton said to me, "Okay, Dan, let's go home." He reversed course heading back to the top of the hill toward the waiting tourists now aiming cameras at Clinton. My worst fear was that he would do what he sometimes did in similar situations, which was to stop and work the crowd. On this day, however, he merely waved at the crowd and continued down the side of the hill back toward Seventeenth Street and the waiting cars. As we descended the hill, upon approaching the supervisor, he again picked up his position with the president and sent me to the trail position, with him completing the run next to POTUS.

I ran a lot with President Clinton in the winter of 1993 as a CAT agent and then beginning during the summer of 1993 as a member of the working shift. The former CAT agents on my shift now consisted of Tony Meeks, Roland McCamis, Joe Clancy, and me. During day shift, we four ran or dressed out to run almost every day. We didn't mind the running. To run with the president of the United States through downtown DC and then have him stop and shake hands with the man on the street was unwise on Clinton's part—dangerous as hell, in fact—and we loved it.

No one on Clinton's staff ever had courage enough to ask him prior to his turning in for the evening if he planned to run the following morning.

As a result, we had to assume that each morning he would run. Each morning we staged a motorcade on the south grounds of the White House outside the diplomatic entrance that led to the area where FDR once gave his "fireside chats"; we were prepared to drive to one of Clinton's favorite running sites. This required the designated runners each morning to show up for shift change in running gear. That, in turn, required the runners to bring their business suits in a hanging bag along with everything else they would need to wear for the day: suit, shirt, belt, socks, shoes, tie, towel, toiletries, and so forth.

As the morning wore on, speculation would always begin as to whether Clinton was going to run or not. Supervisors were put in a bind because they had to make the call after a certain point whether to keep agents in running gear or have them change out into PPD business attire for an upcoming move out of the White House.

When the elevator outside the family residence lit up, everyone knew the president was on his way down. If he were in business attire, we would sprint to our command post area, known as W-16, where we would change from running gear into our suits faster than supermodels changing outfits between runs down the catwalk. There would be shorts and T-shirts flying everywhere as we tried to get into our work attire as quickly as possible. If the president emerged from the elevator in running gear, we all abandoned our posts and fled toward the motorcade, where we would get into the follow-up vehicle behind the limo and drive to the running site, such as the reflecting pool or the Washington Mall.

On one such morning, we were, as usual, standing our posts in running gear. It was getting late, almost nine o'clock, and still no President Clinton. The shift leader, feeling it was safe to do so, made the call for all runners to go ahead and change out for a regular workday into our suits. We changed out and had no sooner assumed our posts when the elevator came down with President Clinton attired in running gear.

He walked to the cars as usual, but there was a problem; there were no cars. The motorcade cars had been cut loose and had returned to their off-site location and could not be recalled in a timely manner. Also, those of us who were runners were in the process of changing from business attire back into running gear. This time there were suit coats, pants, belts, and all manner of masculine wardrobe flying around the command post as if there were a windstorm.

Clinton was not happy to find there were no cars waiting for him. He told the detail leader he wanted to run and off-site and right now. The flustered agent suggested to the president that he run on the never-used track until we could put together some sort of motorcade package. With a look of frustration and without speaking, Clinton began running on the track. Using the emergency motorcade cars staged on the grounds and setting a record for changing outfits, there were cars and agents ready to go before Clinton had run two laps around the quarter-mile track. The Service is above all else a can-do agency. We proceeded to the reflecting pool, which was less than a quarter mile from the White House, and Clinton got in his run.

After returning from a run, the running agents had but a few minutes to grab their suits and bags and get over to the showers located across West Executive Avenue in the Old Executive Office Building.

After running three and sometimes four miles in ninety-degree, 100 percent Washington, DC, humidity, the body does not stop sweating immediately, but rather takes an hour or more. We would take cold showers, jump into our suits, and double-time back to the White House, where we would stand post still sweating as if we had run the three miles in our suits. We were soaked and literally sweating through our clothes. It was miserable, but it was for the leader of the free world and we were getting paid, so what the hell. The rub was that the agents who did not run had to double up on their time on post while we runners were out of the rotation showering and getting dressed, so they received no downtime until we returned.

Clinton always enjoyed an end-of-the-summer trip to Martha's Vineyard, Massachusetts, where for a couple of weeks he played golf and hung out with his friends and wealthy supporters, such as Vernon Jordan, James Taylor, Carly Simon, and the beautiful people of show business. It was a nice place to visit and far more expensive than most agents could ever afford if they went on their own. I went on two occasions and always enjoyed it. Clinton was relaxed and easy work at the vineyard. He also loved to run while there.

While at Martha's Vineyard, I was on the afternoon shift, four o'clock to midnight. One morning I had risen around nine o'clock after staying up a bit too late the night before. I got up, pounded back a lot of water to relieve my state of dehydration, and then went for a five-mile run.

In the afternoon, I walked out of the hotel and into the waiting shift change van that would take us to the POTUS's location to begin our shift. Inside, Bob Byers, the shift leader, was visibly upset. "Hey, Bob," I said, "what's wrong?"

He nearly shouted, "POTUS did not run this morning; he is going to run this afternoon! Someone needs to go get running gear!" No one moved. I said, "Okay, what the hell." I had already run five miles that morning, but if the president of the United States needed an agent to run with him, I estimated that in my current condition I would still do as well as anyone else who might be available. We made the shift change, and as predicted, the president ran, and I ran too. As always, I was happy and proud to be there.

The Running Military Aide

One of the most bizarre parts of the running drama was the fact that the military aides all insisted on running too. Their participation in the run was totally unnecessary and added to the confusion that already existed, but they were all looking for that magic photo op of them running with the POTUS, the commander in chief of the armed forces and their boss.

The military office at the White House assigned as an aide to POTUS one field-grade officer from each branch of the military; that is, an officer with the rank of major, lieutenant commander, or higher. There were then five of them, one each from the army, navy, air force, coast guard, and Marine Corps. These were all high rollers who would one day become generals or admirals, and POTUS was their actual commanding officer, who wrote their evaluations.

One of the major duties of these officers was to carry a large, heavy briefcase known as the "football." As is well known by all, the football contains the nuclear codes and sequence needed by POTUS to start a thermonuclear war and end all civilization. One of these officers and the football travel everywhere POTUS does, and each military aide, of course, took this responsibility very seriously.

Each morning, the military aide on duty would appear in his running outfit, usually adorned in his alma mater's logo of West Point, Annapolis, or the Air Force Academy. He would be dutifully in possession of the football and waiting for the official word on whether the run was a go or no-go. If the run were a go, the military aide rode with the Secret Service in the rear of the follow-up to the running site. Upon reaching the running site, POTUS would emerge from the limo and begin stretching, and the running formation would assume its positions. The run would then begin, military aide and all. There was only one thing missing: the football.

Since it was impractical to run with the thing, the military aides abandoned the codes to World War III in the back of the follow-up vehicle to be watched over by the agent there. We always thought it was a bit risky, but it was the military's responsibility, not ours. I can assure you, however, that should the football have gone missing, the Secret Service—not the future flag-rank officers of the military—would have taken the blame publicly.

Taking blame for things it is not responsible for where presidential staff is concerned has always been an unofficial collateral duty of the Service. This includes the White House-crashing incident, where two Washington socialites were admitted to a White House Christmas party but were not on the guest list. Whenever staff needs a scapegoat for one of their mistakes, the Service has always provided a convenient target. While publicly the Service will accept responsibility for such incidents as the White House gate-crashers, privately the president and staff are well aware of who is actually responsible.

An Assassination That Almost Was

Aside from not having enough running agents, the biggest problem with Clinton's fitness program was that he liked to run in areas where any assassin could lurk, as could a random demented person with a gun. We ran through crowds, crossed city streets, and stood in the open for minutes

**Donnelle and I with President Clinton at the
White House Christmas party, 1994**

(Courtesy of the White House)

at a time by the limo while Clinton stretched before and after the run, all of this with normal traffic flowing by. In spite of our urgings to him that we should not stay in one place too long, he always took his time, as if he were just a normal anonymous citizen.

We also violated the most nonnegotiable rules for security in such matters. We usually left the White House at the same time each day using the same gate and seldom varied our running sites or routes. We had four running venues and did not mix them up very well. We were an assassination waiting to happen. Were it not for an overseas trip, an attempted assassination in all probability would have happened.

During December 1993, Clinton left Washington for two weeks and traveled to Russia. This was the trip where I flew home on the backup plane after shaking hands with Lurch, the Russian security officer. Meanwhile, in Florida there existed a man who a jury decided threatened to kill the president. His basic plan was determined to have been to drive from Orlando, Florida, to Washington, where he would wait along one of our running routes and kill President Clinton as he ran by. It was speculated, also, that he wished to die during the attack in a hail of Secret Service pistol lead.

The location where this individual is said to have sat day after day for over a week was indeed on a route we used regularly. The would-be assassin failed to realize, however, that POTUS was out of the country and would not be by anytime soon. Eventually growing tired of waiting in the cold, he returned to Florida, where he confided what he had done to a friend who then contacted authorities. The suspect was arrested, and in May 1994, was convicted in US District Court of 18 USC 871, threatening the life of the president. He then served four years in federal prison.

As a result of this incident and others not publicly revealed, the Service was finally successful in persuading Clinton to stop the insanity of running in public. Clinton had pushed his and our luck long enough and we had gotten away with it, but all knew that luck would not hold out forever. It seemed to all of us who protected him that it was difficult for Clinton to admit he was not admired by everyone and there were actually those who would kill him were it not for the Secret Service.

Not long after the incident with the potential assassin from Orlando, the running issues were all resolved literally overnight when, at professional golfer Greg Norman's house in Florida, President Clinton caught his heel on a step and fell, tearing his knee. His running days were all but over, and he confined his fitness efforts to the White House, where he used a treadmill and stair-climber.

The next president, George W. Bush, was not a jogger, but an honest-to-God runner. He ran at a six-minute-per-mile pace normally for three miles, and there were even fewer agents who could run with him than with Clinton. Fortunately, W never ran in public, but rather at Camp David or the Secret Service training center in Beltsville, Maryland, where it was much easier to protect him. There is, however, no such thing as a completely safe site, and although using more secure running sites required fewer agents to run with W, there still existed the need for some agents who could keep up with the six-minute pace. As with Clinton, most of those men were current or former CAT agents.

Driving the President

In December 1993, President Clinton was vacationing for a few days in Hilton Head, South Carolina, where he spent most days playing golf and running on the beach. I was doing the advance for the rented house on the beach he was staying in and also managing the command post located at another rented house next door to his. These houses were located in a very affluent neighborhood on a short street with only one way in and one way out, making things easy to secure. Toward the end of the week, my shift leader said he wanted to talk to me in private.

My shift leader and I met in an empty room of the command post, where he commended me on doing a good job with the site. Then he asked which of the other sections of PPD I would like to go to, meaning First Lady detail or transportation section. Since CAT had been a section of PPD since 1992, I pointed out the obvious: that I had recently come from CAT and my section time had therefore been satisfied. He agreed with my logic but stated that agents were needed to drive the president or to move to the First Lady's detail. I told my shift leader to assign me wherever I could be best utilized.

Upon returning from Hilton Head, I had the weekend off and then reported for work at the White House on Monday. It was a normal day at the White House, and I was standing post in the main mansion when Danny Spriggs, the ASAIC of manpower, approached. Danny had played college football at the University of New Mexico and was then drafted by the Dallas Cowboys prior to becoming an agent. He smiled his usual large smile and then informed me that I would be moved from the shift to transportation section the following Monday. There I would become one of a select few who would drive the president of the United States in an armored limousine, drive the working shift in the follow-up vehicle, and plan presidential motorcades.

Over the next several months, I drove President Clinton scores of times, both in the United States and in other countries. The mission was twofold: One, of course, was to safely drive the president from point A to point B. The other was to do whatever was necessary, using skills perfected in protective operations driver's school, to move the president out of a kill zone should the motorcade be attacked. We who drove the president were anything but chauffeurs. We were all agents, moving our protective skills from walking and running alongside the president to a new dimension that included safely transporting him in a vehicle specifically designed to increase the chances of his survival in an attack.

The limousines we drove were very large and very heavy. In spite of their 450-cubic-inch engines, there was lag time between depressing the accelerator and the car beginning to move. Conversely one had to begin braking well in advance of the point where the car was expected to stop. Because President Clinton never wore a seat belt, a driver always had to be constantly thinking ahead of the car and the situation in order to avoid disaster.

To be selected as one of the agents tasked with the obviously huge responsibility of driving the president was an honor, although I was not in a hurry to leave my shift. My main concern, however, was that although I had graduated from the driving course that qualified an agent to drive an armored limousine years earlier, I had not driven one since 1989 and was in bad need of some refresher training. I voiced this concern to ASAIC Danny Spriggs, who assured me I would have the chance to train on the newer, larger limousines prior to my first time driving the president.

In spite of Danny's assurances that I would have time to get some familiarization time in one of these hulking giants before driving POTUS, it never happened. In one week, with no refresher training, I would find myself driving a full-size armored limo containing the entire Clinton family at night through a blinding rainstorm.

Valentine's Day 1994 was a miserably cold, rain-soaked day in Washington. It was one of my first days in the transportation section, and I was still waiting for my familiarization time with the full-size armored limousines. I was assigned the 2:00 p.m. to 10:00 p.m. shift, along with agent Mike Wilson, who had several months experience in the transportation section. There was nothing on POTUS's schedule for the night, and it looked like it would be a quiet evening of paperwork and making telephone calls to anyone you wanted. It did not turn out that way.

At around eight o'clock, the phone rang in the transportation section office. On the other end was the shift leader of the president's detail. He announced that POTUS wanted to go to Andrews Air Force Base and surprise Hillary, whose airplane was scheduled to arrive in two hours. I was to drive the limo.

This should have been an easy assignment, only I would be driving a car as big as a medium-size boat that I had never set foot in, with POTUS as my passenger. Because Mike Wilson was the senior agent, he did the advance work of making the notifications to the support authorities, such as Metro Police; I went downstairs to where the POTUS's operational vehicles were kept and prepped the limo, making sure it was ready. I would have about five minutes to familiarize myself with this car's peculiar handling characteristics. Unfortunately, it would not be on the driving course at the training center, but driving to the White House from the garage.

We arrived at the White House, and my mentor, agent Mike Wilson, disappeared to meet with his police counterpart. I was alone in the dark, sitting in the belly of the beast, which smelled like it had just come from the car wash, as all protective vehicles do.

As I sat, I pondered the fact that I was about to drive the president of the United States at night in some of the worst rain imaginable in an off-the-record motorcade with no intersection control—all so he could surprise his wife on Valentine's Day. He obviously had a great deal of confidence in us all.

The sound and movement of the right rear door of the beast being opened broke my trance. In stepped the president's daughter, Chelsea, and the president, who both greeted me with, "Hi." Clinton was familiar with me from our runs over the past year and my working with him for the past six months. He actually knew most of his agents by name, including me, having a near if not totally photographic memory. I responded with, "Good evening, Mr. President," and then nodded at Chelsea. The thought now occurred to me that on the way back from Andrews, should we actually make it that far without me rear-ending the lead car, the First Lady would also be in the backseat.

The right rear door closed, and the detail leader opened the right front door, greeting me with, "Hi, Dan," as he settled into his seat. This particular supervisor could be a bear and was prone to chewing large chunks of rear end from unsuspecting agents with no notice. He always did it in a gentlemanly way, and it was never personal. I had somehow avoided it until now, but the possibility always existed. I felt, given the circumstances this evening, that it was not only possible, but also quite probable.

Over my earpiece connected to the Secret Service car radio, I heard the voice of the shift leader calling the shift into the follow-up vehicle directly behind us. The marked police lead car began to move, and the detail leader looked at me and said, "Let's go." Off we went into the abyss.

The first obstacle to overcome leaving the south grounds of the White House was a set of serpentine barriers. Even with practice, of which I had none, I viewed it as a virtual impossibility to not run over the damned things, but somehow I managed not to. The idea was to not jostle POTUS any more than necessary, although I was more concerned with not crashing the limo containing the president of the United States. We left behind the security and lights of the White House and then headed off into the ink-black night.

Driving less than a car length behind the lead car, staring at its taillights in the rain while looking through what appeared to be a fishbowl with windshield wipers, took every ounce of concentration I had. In addition to visual concentration, I also had to listen to my friend Mike Wilson in the lead car requesting lane changes to the follow-up. When Mike saw a lane shift was needed, he would call out his request to the follow-up. Once I heard "clear" from the follow-up, I would automatically make the lane change without ever taking my eyes off the taillights of the lead. The limo driver had to have complete trust and confidence in the follow-up, and I did.

With no intersection control, we were moving with the flow of traffic, and it was tense. Along the way to Andrews Air Force Base (AAFB), which was about a thirty-minute drive in this weather, we saw several accidents; the flashing lights of the emergency vehicles on site refracted off the prisms of raindrops on the fishbowl, making things even more distorted. I had to keep my eyes constantly moving, from the taillights of the lead car to my panel (I had the rheostat turned almost all the way down) and then back up to avoid fixation on the lights and spatial disorientation. It was essential to keep this scan going, or you could easily crash into the lead, which was continually speeding up and slowing down with the traffic. After about thirty very exciting minutes, we arrived at AAFB and proceeded down an access road through a gate manned by an agent and out onto the tarmac to stage and await the C-9 aircraft bearing Hillary Rodham Clinton, first lady of the United States.

The four of us sat in the limo—POTUS, Chelsea, the detail leader, and me. POTUS and the detail leader had a cordial conversation as we waited. POTUS had brought a bouquet of flowers for his wife and seemed happy and excited to surprise her. In the end, presidents are not much different from any other husband or father, I suppose.

Upon hearing on the radio that Hillary's aircraft had landed, we started engines and prepared to move onto the tarmac. The blue and white

Douglas C-9 with the emblazoned wording "United States of America" on the fuselage taxied into the bright lights set up to illuminate the arrival for the media, who were standing by in their press pen.

The air force pilot in command applied brakes to this gorgeous product of the American aviation industry until he brought the aircraft to a full stop. We then moved the cars up to the plane, with the president's door on the right side facing the aircraft. As the door of the plane opened, a motorized ladder was placed alongside. Hillary emerged and descended the steps, waving to the press, not yet realizing the cars waiting for her were the president's. When she was about halfway down the steps, President Clinton and Chelsea exited the limo. POTUS stood there holding the flowers with a kind of happy look on his face like any other husband hoping to pleasantly surprise his wife. It was apparent that Hillary was very surprised indeed at his appearance.

Hillary and Bill entered the rear of the limo with Chelsea between them, the door was closed, and we departed back to the White House. Along the way, Hillary commented to Bill how surprised she was to see him. I tuned it out and concentrated on my sole purpose in life, which was delivering them all safely back to the White House.

By now I was feeling a lot more confident in my ability to safely drive the beast, and the return trip to the White House went without incident. The last major hurdle was guiding the limo around the barriers in reverse order and getting the thing back onto the south grounds of the White House without launching the president, First Lady, and Chelsea into the front seat.

We arrived in front of the entrance to the south portico, where I brought the beast to a stop so gently the feeling of transitioning from motion to a stop was scarcely noticeable. The detail leader whispered, "Thanks, Dan," and exited the car. I heard the right rear door open and President Clinton and Chelsea saying, "Thank you," which I later discovered was always their habit. Hillary exited in silence. I replied, "My pleasure," and breathed a heavy sigh of relief. With the leader of the free world and his family once again safely home, Mike Wilson and I cranked up the limo and follow-up, and then headed back to the garage. But first the limo had to be refueled.

If a limo's fuel supply fell to three quarters, it was standard procedure to get the tank topped off, as the possibility always existed that an emergency could occur during a motorcade and force you to drive POTUS for a couple hundred miles. These armored limos only got about eight to ten miles a gallon as it was, and were nearly fuel-critical from the time you pulled away from the pump.

When in Washington, we normally frequented a station in a socioeconomically deprived area not far from where we stored the cars. It was always a show when we would arrive to fuel up. Everyone in this particular neighborhood knew who we were and who rode in the car we were fueling. So there you would be, standing at the self-service pump putting 93-octane gas into the president's limo at a station in the hood.

A 1993 Cadillac armored limousine first used by President Clinton. This vehicle sported a 450-cubic-inch engine. The actual weight is classified.

(Courtesy of the White House)

The local residents loved it when we would arrive to fuel the limo and always liked to come out and watch. I would not have chosen this particular station to fuel my family Volvo, but we always felt safe there. Everyone knew we were armed, undoubtedly dangerous, and would have no qualms about protecting the limo by any means necessary.

In those days, the president's operational cars were kept in a nondescript building located at 1310 L Street in Washington. The outside of the building during the daylight hours was a normal-looking area, with citizens going about their business. After nightfall, it became hooker alley. There were so many working girls standing around in front of the building, you sometimes had to wade through them to get inside the place.

When we would depart with the spare limo, limo, and follow-up, the girls would practically line the streets and cheer as we passed on our way to the White House. They constantly asked if they could have a ride in the POTUS's limo. We all said no to that one, as we valued our jobs far too much.

Feeling the Strain

When new presidents enter the White House, they tend to travel little. The early part of a new administration is spent with everyone, including the president, learning the routine. Once things settle down a bit, new presidents discover the marvel known as Air Force One and begin to use it extensively, each seeming to feel the need to make more trips, foreign and domestic, than his predecessor. When Bill Clinton finally discovered he could travel anywhere he wished, anytime he wished, he began to exercise that privilege with total abandon.

During the early days of the Clinton administration, we did not have nearly enough agents to cover his almost impossible travel schedule. I, along with most other agents on PPD, began working up to thirty days at a time with no days off for months on end, and in my case for over five years, including the Bush presidency. I had finally begun to feel the strain from the excitement and fun of protecting the president lapse into a job performed at times while so fatigued, I scarcely knew what day it was.

I had reported to CAT in 1989 with the mission of protecting the president of the United States. While presidential protection was one of the most important jobs in the world and I still received a great deal of satisfaction from the work, by 1994 it had begun to weigh on me more than anytime in the past. I had now reached the point where, although still on my game, I was not as sharp as I had once been. This phenomenon is common among almost all PPD agents after about four years of continuous protection, and I was one year beyond that. This is not a good condition for an agent assigned to protect the president to be in.

One morning I was home enjoying a rare day off when the phone rang. It was agent Carter Kim from transportation operations directing me to leave immediately for a trip where I was to do the advance. For the first time in my career, I verbally removed the head of the messenger delivering bad news.

After apologizing to Carter for my out-of-line comment, I hung up the phone and began to pack for yet another trip. I had been the operations agent in CAT for several months during my four years there and knew all too well the discomfort of calling an agent at home to inform him he was going to have to leave unexpectedly for a trip. Carter had a difficult job, and I had not helped make it any easier.

In the life of a PPD agent, the interruption of one's routine to go on a trip is normal, and up until now, I would have merely acknowledged the instructions and begun preparing for the trip. This case was different, however, since in addition to being mentally and physically exhausted from five years of such phone calls, I had just returned from a long and particularly stressful foreign trip. My frustration was enhanced by the fact that this new excursion, which would cost the taxpayer a fortune, amounted to nothing more than a recreational trip for the president in my opinion.

Ripping Carter was out of character for me and alerted me to the fact that I was becoming saturated with both physical and emotional chronic fatigue that no amount of sleep could remedy. Only permanent removal from the situation causing the condition would resolve the issue.

Everyone on the detail during this period was becoming irritable from the nonstop travel. Resentment was beginning to build toward management, who did not appear to feel that more people were needed on the detail and seemed unconcerned about the unrealistic work schedules. The Secret Service mantra of "just make it work" was wearing thin.

I had now been in the transportation section for almost a year and had been protecting presidents on a full-time basis for over five years. As my tour was coming to an end in the transportation section, thus signaling my return to the working shift, I asked for transfer from PPD to the Atlanta field office. I gave the reason for my request as wanting to return to an office close to my home of record.

The actual reason was due, more than anything else, to the fact I was approaching burnout and could feel it getting closer with each passing day. I needed, at least for the time being, to get out of protection and do something different in order to regain perspective on life and my career. I did not admit my condition to anyone, including my wife, for saying burnout aloud in the Secret Service was total career suicide.

The following week I was told by Willis Johnson, the new ASAIC of manpower, that I was being transferred, per my wishes, but to the Washington field office (WFO) rather than the Atlanta office. I was to replace my wife, who was an agent there, and she would replace me on PPD. The Washington field office was the last place I wanted to be assigned, and I preferred to remain on PPD until I could make the move to Atlanta.

In a total funk, I went home and telephoned the new SAIC of PPD, Lew Merletti, to let him know that until I could secure a spot in Atlanta, I wanted to remain on PPD. He informed me it was too late and that my transfer was final. I told Lew that if I had to leave the detail and could not move to Atlanta, I would prefer another assignment besides WFO. Lew said he could have me assigned to the training division as an instructor, and after some additional discussion, I accepted the assignment.

After being an agent for eleven years, I realized that, while protecting the president was still the most important thing the Secret Service did, it was not the only important thing. I also realized that presidential protection was something a person could not do indefinitely, with even the strongest having their limits. There were many other vital jobs to be performed, and training the new group of young people who wished to become agents was critically important. I had enjoyed my years on CAT and PPD more than

I can accurately describe, and although I was not going to Atlanta, I was going to a worthwhile assignment where I could perhaps pass on some of the knowledge I had acquired to others.

I checked out of PPD on a Friday, and my wife replaced me, checking in the following Monday. At the same time she was putting her things in my old cubby located inside the White House Command Post W-16, I was checking into the Special Agent Training Education Division, or SATED for short, then located at 1310 L street, where over the following nine years, I would have a part in training over two thousand new Secret Service agents.

CHAPTER 12

Shaping the Next Generation

I n the late fall of 1994, I left PPD and reported to the Special Agent Training Education Division (SATED), where I would become an instructor teaching special agent students, as well as offering refresher training for the major protective details. SATED was divided into two basic sections: protection and investigations. Most of the investigations syllabus was taught by agents who had not served on PPD, while the protection syllabus was reserved for those who had either PPD or Vice Presidential Protective Division (VPPD) experience. Due to my having served on PPD, including the shift, CAT, and the transportation section, I was logically assigned to teach protection.

Most of the agents arriving from protection were like me, near burnouts that needed some downtime. Most of us had zero experience teaching anything, and there was no way to know if a person could or could not teach until it was too late to change things. As a result, many relied heavily on slides and PowerPoint and were boring instructors. That also described me at first.

The important thing was to be able to teach from a position of having done in real time what you were teaching. I found that the new students would automatically give you the attention and respect deserved, as long as you had actually performed the subject matter in a genuine setting. These were not children, but adults, who in many cases had vast law enforcement and military experience and could spot a fraud miles away.

Each class of twenty-four students was assigned two course coordinators, who stayed with the class for the entire ten weeks the class was in Washington for the Special Agent Training Course (SATC) and also monitored the class while it was in the Federal Law Enforcement Training Center (FLETC) during the ten weeks there. These two instructors were to be the mentors, role models, and proctors for each class. Like most things, it was a job that a person could put as much or as little into it as he wanted. I saw it as a great chance to influence the young people who would become the future of the Service. While some instructors took it seriously, some looked at it as a bother because it was so time-consuming.

The classes were only given to instructors who had been around for a while, so although I wanted a class, I knew it would be a while before I had the seniority. While waiting my turn at being a course coordinator, I taught all courses in the protection syllabus, but due to the numbers of classes arriving and too few instructors, I was to receive my own class much earlier than anticipated. I received my first class as a course coordinator during the spring of 1995, just a few months after my arrival in training.

My observation of other classes and their coordinators was that the classes were too laid-back, with almost no discipline. Instead of leaders and mentors, many coordinators wanted to be buddies with their charges. The result was loss of respect and discipline and a general feeling of disorganization. These classes were sloppy, ill-kempt, and acted as if they had already graduated. My most notable observation was there was no leadership by example during the mandatory physical training (PT) sessions. That is, the coordinators were sitting in the office while the physical training instructors handled the class. Some coordinators cancelled PT altogether because of weather.

All of this was about to change with my class and cause me to alienate some, but win the respect of the students, reluctant admiration from some colleagues, and an epiphany from some that this was the way training should be conducted.

Contrary to the accusations and reminders of many in the training division, I knew we were in the Secret Service and not the Marine Corps—painfully aware on most days. Few days went by without some wizard training genius saying, "Dan, this is not the Marine Corps." I would thank them for their keen insight, acknowledge that I was aware of this fact, and drive on. I believed, however, that many of the same principles used to produce marine officers could also be effectively used to produce outstanding Secret Service agents. There was an acceptable median between the world of extreme military training and the Secret Service, and I would find it.

I was assigned to be the course coordinator for Special Agent Training Class 138, which would arrive in the late spring of 1995. My assistant coordinator, John Mrha, was a good friend and my former assistant team leader in CAT when I was new there. Like me, he was a military veteran, but unlike me, he was a great athlete.

John had gone from CAT to PPD to Training Division as had I and was a hard-liner like me, but in a quieter way. John looked a lot like the actors Montgomery Clift and Richard Gere combined, and people liked him for his competence, good looks, and charm. We were a good team and agreed that our class would be made intelligent, disciplined, and fit, and that we would run the class along the same lines as police academies and the military. We also were in firm agreement that we would not require our class to participate in any physical training unless we were leading them.

SATC 138

The new class that would become SATC 138 arrived in June 1995 for the Special Agent Introductory Training Course (SAITC). SAITC was a one-week course of instruction where the new class reported for initial indoctrination and weapons familiarization prior to going to FLETC for ten weeks. They would then return to Washington, where John and I would have them for ten weeks prior to graduation.

SAITC was a chance for John and me to introduce ourselves to our new class and lay out what we expected of them. It was also a chance for us to conduct some preliminary evaluations of what we had to work with. I made it very clear what we expected: total effort at all times no matter what the endeavor was. Anything less than 100 percent in any area would be rewarded with a ticket home. We also promised to always lead them in all physical activities.

At the end of the first day, John and I gave the fitness test to our new class. The test consisted of pull-ups, sit-ups, push-ups, flexibility, and the one-and-a-half-mile run. Most did okay, and at the end of the run, they thought they were finished. Not! After the run, John and I formed up the class and ran them another several miles.

At the end of the additional running, we informed the class to always expect the unexpected, that this was the easiest day they would have, and that if anyone did not think they could hack it, now would be a good time to be man or woman enough to say so and go home. There were no takers, although there were one or two I thought looked unpromising.

Following one week of SAITC, the class left for FLETC in Georgia for ten weeks of the criminal investigators training program (CITP), and probably thought they had seen the last of us for a while.

John and I flew down to Brunswick, Georgia, one day to surprise them, let them know we were always close at hand, check on their welfare, make sure FLETC was not unfairly harassing any of them, and take them for an impromptu fitness session.

FLETC had its own fitness program, but it was substandard to the Secret Service program in every way. The FLETC sessions were too infrequent, meaning not held every day, and not intense enough to produce tangible results. It was more of a wellness program (I hate the mere term). Most of the FLETC fitness instructors lead the runs from a golf cart, where they yell at students over a PA system rather than run with them. I had come to realize at this point that leadership by example in its formal sense was exclusive to the military and almost anyone who was not a military veteran had no more idea what it meant than I could understand quantum physics.

While at FLETC, Secret Service students are under the control of FLETC, not the Secret Service, so upon arriving John and I had to make contact with the FLETC fitness coordinator who was responsible for the class our students were in. John and I found him, with gut protruding over his shorts and having a smoke outside the PT building before class. John and I informed him who we were and that we intended to take the Secret Service part of his class for a freelance session. We did not really ask if it would be okay; we just said we were going to do it. He was hesitant as he smoked his cigarette, but we prevailed.

After his class of forty-eight, including our twenty-four Secret Service students, formed up, John and I appeared, much to the visible sorrow of our people, and took the Secret Service students for a "tour of the complex." We began the run at approximately three thirty. At four thirty, we were still going.

After over one hour of running in what had to be ninety-degree heat, we stopped at the main fitness building to allow the class a water break, in which John and I did not partake. They were proud that they had run a solid hour without stopping, many never having run that far and not believing they could. There was only one problem: to everyone's disbelief, the run was not over.

Upon returning to the parking lot from the comfort of the air-conditioned fitness building and the cold-water dispenser, the class formed up. We spoke to the class briefly about the importance of mental hardness and told them that the body could take a hell of a lot more than most thought. We then informed them that now that we were warmed up, we could begin the PT session. You could hear the panic jump from most of them. I invited anyone who did not want to continue the session to pack for the trip home. All elected to continue.

We did not run much longer. The second session was really an attitude check to see if anyone would quit or balk. No one did, but an incident did occur that today remains the topic of humorous discussion anytime I have the honor of talking to a former member of 138.

We had gone about ten more minutes after the water break when a student began to moan and cry. I asked the distressed young man what the problem was. He shouted back at me, "I am tired and it hurts!" That was, as you might imagine, not the correct response. Actually any response other than "nothing is wrong" would have been incorrect. I informed him and the rest of the class that we would practice being tired for a little while longer, until the young man stopped his disgusting display of emotion and began to act like an agent.

Concerned we might be on the verge of permanently damaging someone, John and I returned the class to the parking lot, where we gave them another water break, with John and I once again abstaining. Upon returning to formation, we told them we were going for yet another run and offered again that anyone not wishing to continue could quit the program now. This was a critical moment, because we knew they were as physically done as we dared make them without putting people in the hospital. The class stared at us with the blank looks of prison camp survivors, but none would quit. Satisfied we had a pretty decent group, we dismissed the class with no further running, much to their delight and relief.

Each student was deservedly proud of his accomplishment that day, and each was a little harder, tougher, and more confident than before. You can also bet that each either called or wrote letters home that evening telling of his triumph over adversity and his two insane coordinators. John and I handed out no compliments that day, however. We let the class know that their job had been to run until John and I decided the run was over, and that no one was going to thank them for doing their job.

It was on this day that the class began to show signs of pulling together as a team and take pride in the fact that, as a class, they had survived what many would have not. They also began to form a bond that can only be formed when a group is subjected to common hardship. That had been our purpose of this brutal session, not because we liked to run for miles in the heat but to build confidence and team.

It also proved to the class that John and I were true to our word and would always lead them, rather than manage them, and that whatever we made them do physically, we would always be in the front. They did not know it yet, but we were teaching them about leadership, teamwork, and what it really meant to be a Secret Service agent. And for the moment, John and I gave them something to dislike (the two of us), which made them an even tighter group.

A few weeks later, 138 returned from FLETC to begin their ten weeks of special agent training in Washington and Beltsville. John and I greeted them upon their return with another sixty-minute run around the complex. This session included running up and down stairs of the hundred-foot rappelling tower until someone became physically ill.

This became a class joke and also the indicator of when we had run the tower enough times. After a few trips to the tower, the class caught on that we would stop running the tower after someone lost lunch. At that point, they decided ahead of time who it would be for each run, and the student would gag himself or herself, thereby reducing the number of trips up the tower. It was all good fun, and the class had a great time with it.

While it may sound strange to some, this type of training helps build camaraderie and aids in the development of "dark humor," which is essential to people in dangerous professions. It is the part of training that teaches a person that, while being concerned with the welfare of others, laughter at misfortune and hardship while continuing onward can partially relieve the pain and stress of the situation.

On days when the class would report to 1310 L Street in Washington for a day of classroom instruction, we would always begin the day with a six o'clock morning run down to the Washington Mall, the Capitol, the Lincoln Memorial, and back, which took about one hour. The sight of the sun rising over the Capitol and the monuments was always moving, and the students seemed to enjoy it. At least they never complained, but then again, complaining was not allowed.

Since John and I lived about thirty miles from downtown Washington, we had to get up earlier than the class, and we did not leave until the class had departed for the day. The class knew this, and leadership by example stopped any complaining before it started, at least from the class. Complaining from other instructors was a different story.

Some instructors complained to John and me that our class was having trouble staying awake during their lectures; they wanted us to ease up and give the students more rest. I told the complaining instructors that if their classes were interesting, the students would not have a problem staying awake. Some complained to management about it, but much to our surprise, management backed us up. It was a sign that at least some of the boys on mahogany row were starting to buy into the program. Many, however, were still watching in quiet disapproval.

John and I were purposely putting the class into sleep deprivation, because Secret Service agents are usually sleep deprived, whether it is on protection or in the field. We were training them to become familiar with fatigue, to overcome it mentally and physically, and then drive on with the mission.

In the real world, agents could not tell the president of the United States they were tired and needed some rest, anymore than they could say to him it was too hot or cold to run. John and I cited to our class that we had run with President Clinton in hundred-degree weather as well as close to zero degrees and that there was a purpose to everything we were subjecting them to. The class was doing well in all areas, especially fitness, but we were beginning to bore them and ourselves to death with standard workouts. It was time to raise the bar.

The Obstacle Course

During the 1980s and until 1997, when the James J. Rowley Training Center (JJRTC) built its own obstacle course, part of CAT training involved running the obstacle course at Fort Meade, Maryland, located about ten miles north of the JJRTC.

This ugly assembly of concrete and pipe was built sometime during World War II. It was several hundred yards long but seemed to go on forever and was laid out in the shape of a horseshoe. Although it was not a part of the SATC syllabus, John and I decided it would be a great morale booster for 138, as well as a hell of a good workout. It had nearly killed me during CAT school in 1988, while John sometimes ran it just for fun.

On a cool November afternoon in 1995, with the leaves on the trees bordering the Baltimore Washington Parkway showing their brilliant colors of red and gold, John and I took 138 to Fort Meade and the awaiting obstacle course. Upon arriving at the obstacle course, John and I first explained to the class the purpose in this training. We emphasized that, in addition to fitness, there was a job-related, practical reason for it. As criminal investigators in field offices, each might very well find themselves in a foot chase with a criminal suspect, and failure to apprehend a suspect due to lack of fitness or the inability to negotiate a wall or fence was unacceptable.

John and I then ran the course together as a team, demonstrating the best, most efficient way to negotiate each obstacle. Then it was their turn.

We started the students off two at a time and directed they finish the course with their partner. After surviving the ordeal, we then sent them through again, this time individually. Some did well, and others looked, as we pointed out, like monkeys trying to mate with a football, but the exercise was a huge success. So much so, in fact, that our boss, Bill Parr, directed that all future classes would undergo the Fort Meade obstacle course.

The problem with this order was that, other than John and I, few other instructors would subject themselves to being checked out on the course. Many felt it beneath them to get dirty with a class, and to put it another way, many were afraid to try because of the risk of being embarrassed in front of a class if they could not negotiate an obstacle. This, in spite of never-ending offers by John and I to show each instructor all the tricks necessary in order to complete each obstacle.

As time went on, I took all SATC classes to the course and demonstrated, while some course directors watched in sheepish discomfort with arms folded. Fatigue makes cowards of us all, and yet due to the "true believers," such as John, Mike Carbone, Scott Marble, Todd Bagby, and a few others, no class failed to be introduced to the obstacle course during my tenure as an instructor.

SATC 138 finally graduated, and at the ceremony, each student resembled recruiting poster-models in their suits, with lean, chiseled faces created from the loss of any unnecessary fat. Awards were presented to students who had distinguished themselves in the areas of academics, firearms, and fitness. When the scores were read for the top fitness award, there was an audible response from the audience. All were amazed at the fitness level of this individual and of the class as a whole.

After graduation had concluded, John and I shook hands with each of our former students, now full-fledged agents, and sent them on their way. Both John and I felt we had done our best to produce the finest agents possible and believed we had succeeded in doing so. While the experience of being a course coordinator had been very rewarding, it had practically

**Here, I am unwisely running the obstacle course against a student
half my age. The class is of course cheering for their colleague.**

(Personal collection of Dan Emmett)

consumed me, and I was ready to begin teaching the standard curriculum once more. This was not to be.

After everyone had left the area following the graduation of 138, Mr. Parr took me aside and said he wanted me to run another class, SATC 141, which would be arriving in the next few months. He said he wanted 141 run exactly the same as 138 and expected another stellar class. I replied, "Yes, sir"; it would be done.

SATC 141

In that all classes were selected from the same basic applicant pool, I had always believed that most classes were more or less the same, with the only difference in class quality and performance being the people who led them. I firmly believed undisciplined coordinators produced undisciplined classes, while disciplined, demanding coordinators produced the best classes. While I continued to believe that throughout my years as an instructor, with Class 141, I came to realize that each class had its own distinct personality. I was also about to learn that, due to the new and yet unknown political sensitivity of Secret Service management at the headquarters level, it would only take one student's groundless complaints of alleged mistreatment to damage careers and most of what had been accomplished in changing the philosophy of training over the past year.

As 141 moved through the SATC syllabus, I ran this class with my new assistant as John and I had run 138, and they progressed much the same, although they were much higher maintenance than 138, with the simplest things sometimes being a struggle. In late July 1996, they were within two weeks of graduating, and I could move on with other things. As I relaxed at home one Sunday evening with a twelve-year-old scotch and cigar fantasizing about 141's graduation and the reclamation of my life, the phone rang.

The voice at the other end was one of our female students, and she sounded upset. In a shaky voice, she told me that she had over the weekend visited the Brunswick/Savannah, Georgia, area and that due to heavy traffic, she had missed her flight back to Washington. She further lamented there were no other flights back to the Washington/Baltimore area until

**SATC 138 at Fort Meade obstacle course, 1995. I am
at the far left. John Mrha is at the far right.**

(Personal collection of Dan Emmett)

the following afternoon. I told her in as calm a voice as I could summon, to report to me when she arrived back the following day.

Upon her arrival the next day, I found an empty office where I firmly counseled her that this glitch was her fault, not the fault of the heavy traffic, and that with the concurrence of the SAIC of training, she was being restricted to the Washington area until graduation. I advised her this consequence was based on the fact she was not yet an agent, but a student who had failed to return to training on time; therefore she was being penalized as any other student would be in the same situation. She continued to try and avoid blame by insisting the incident was due to the heavy traffic, and she continued to display an openly defiant attitude. This led me to the inescapable conclusion that my constant teachings to special agent trainees regarding accepting responsibility for one's actions were apparently lost on her.

With the graduation of 141 nearing and having so many other issues regarding the class to concentrate on, I put the incident behind me; I had forgotten about it, in fact, although our student apparently had not. The following day, I was going through some paperwork when I received a call from Mr. Parr directing me to proceed to his office.

With a pained expression similar to that of someone reporting the death of a loved one, he informed me that my tardy, unrepentant student had called her SAIC to complain about being disciplined for her still-unacknowledged mistake of leaving for the airport too late. The bombshell of her complaint, however, was the claim I had "harassed" her by being tougher on her than others in her class. She also accused my assistant and me of imposing excessive physical fitness training on the class.

Had she used any other word than "harassed," her complaints might very well have died on the spot. The hard reality, however, was that she did use the word, and not only would this situation not die—it now had a life of its own.

Unbeknownst to everyone outside of headquarters, the Service was in the process of moving into a new chapter of gender-related sensitivity. In this chapter, a vacuum was created between the old Service, where few complaints from any student would have been entertained, and the new Service, where one female student making hollow accusations would result in an immediate rush to judgment against those accused. Both my assistant and I were pulled into that vacuum and then dropped into the perfect storm of the emerging political correctness of the 1990s that had overtaken the entire US government since the infamous navy Tailhook scandal. In this new era, the word "harassment," when used by a female, had become one of the most powerful weapons any female could use against a male. By using the "H" word, our student set off a series of events that could not be recalled even by her, and as a result was awarded instant "victim" status by a Secret Service that was beginning to bear little resemblance to the one I joined in 1983.

While our student had merely alleged that she had been singled out for punishment, everyone who was aware of the situation assumed because a female had lodged the complaint that we were being accused of sexual harassment, which was never the case. The fact she had failed to return to training on time or at the earliest possible time after missing her flight seemed to go selectively unnoticed by some. It was also apparent that she either sensed or was informed of the change in the social paradigm of the Service as she continued to perfect her role of victim.

Although initially too naive at the time to realize it, she was a victim, but not from any action by my assistant or me. In the end, she was a victim of her own frivolous complaint, after which certain high-level managers used her as a pawn to demonstrate the new world order of the Secret Service.

Inspection

As a result of our student's accusations, the assistant director of training, who had only weeks prior congratulated me for a job well done with 138, ordered a formal investigation or inspection of the verbal allegations by our student against me and my assistant.

After countless interviews conducted by agents from the Office of Inspection with all students in the class, as well as my assistant and me, the inspection finally ended with the submission of the final report to the assistant director of training. The official findings of the six-month inquisition by the Office of Inspection were: **"No evidence was found to support the accusations of individual harassment or the imposing of excessive physical training."** The matter was now officially closed.

Although found not guilty of all complaints, my assistant and I were both now perceived to be antifemale by certain members of the director's staff, meaning the radical feminists who had begun to play a major role in the running of the Secret Service. This absurd perception was made even more ridiculous by the fact my assistant and I were both married to Secret Service agents.

During the course of the inspection and subsequent to 141's graduation, I continued to teach physical training and the protection syllabus to all SATC classes. As always, I did my best to prepare these young men and women to survive in a nonpolitically correct world, where there is no gender norming. In that world, there are those who would kill a person because that person carries a badge, and none of these predators care if the carrier of the badge were a man or a woman. I remained determined that no student under my instruction and leadership would ever meet such a fate because I had not done enough to prepare them.

America at War

On September 11, 2001, Al Qaeda attacked the United States, killing over three thousand Americans. One result of this act of war was the Secret Service hired agents in record numbers to fill hundreds of newly authorized slots. I realized that due to the numbers involved and the shortage of instructors, I would probably be made course coordinator yet again, although I hoped otherwise. In the five years since the inspection, per my request I had not been given another class as a coordinator and was quite satisfied to merely teach the protection and fitness syllabus.

One day in 2002, my concern was realized. After returning from taking a class for a run, my ASAIC, Pat Caldwell, dropped by my office. The purpose of his visit was to tell me that due to the high number of classes now being trained, it was necessary for me to be assigned as the course coordinator for the next class coming aboard. He also informed me that the son of the director of the United States Secret Service would be a member of this group. In spite of my initial trepidation over having the director's son in my class, Ben Stafford, son of then-director Brian Stafford, turned out to be one of the best students I ever trained.

Taking a class for a six-mile run

(Personal collection of Dan Emmett)

This class finished their training with no major incidents, other than the usual complaints from some about the perceived severity of the fitness program. After their graduation, I went about my regular instructor duties and forgot about them. With eight years in training and nearly two thousand students under or over the bridge, it was easy to forget a class the minute they walked out the door, and all students were beginning to look exactly alike to me.

Promotion and Return to PPD

One uneventful day in 2002, I was teaching a class when Pat Caldwell, the ASAIC, walked into my classroom and announced that I had been promoted to GS-14, assistant to the special agent in charge (ATSAIC) in the Division of Training. He then walked out and left me with my class. While I was happy to finally be promoted, I had not really been expecting this good news and was a bit in shock over the matter for the remainder of the class, as well as the remainder of the day.

It was now 2002, and being eligible for retirement in one more year, I decided to try and get back to PPD for one last operational assignment. I had spent far too long as an instructor, and like an actor too long in one role, had been typecast. Many believed I had been away from the operational side of the house for so long that teaching was all I was capable of. Perhaps they were right, but I wanted the chance to find out.

In August 2003, I requested and was selected for reassignment back to PPD as one of two supervisors in charge of CAT. After a nine-year absence, I was returning to protection.

CHAPTER 13

Retirement

November 2003 found me reporting back to PPD and CAT after a prolonged absence from the world of operational life. For the past nine years, I had taught others how to protect presidents and get and stay in shape. Now I was back helping to accomplish the most important mission in the Secret Service, which of course is protecting the president of the United States.

On my first day back at PPD, a supervisors' meeting was held by Eddie Marinzel, the SAIC of PPD. As I walked into the meeting, I was greeted by legions of old friends now in charge of the detail. It was a "who's who" of the best agents in protection, as well as the Secret Service. These were the men I had started the job with in 1983, traveled the world with, and respected greatly. Most were former CAT teammates and PPD shift mates, and I could see the president was in good hands.

Although back on PPD and occasionally managing to get out of the office with a team, my new job was essentially administrative. I was one of two ATSAICs in the CAT program and was in charge of managing six of the twelve teams. Managing, not leading. The real leaders were the team leaders at the GS-13 level. Here lay the trade-off between being a line agent and a supervisor.

While most agents, including myself, aspired to at least the GS-14 rank, I discovered that even with the extra money, perks, and privileges that came with higher rank, being a working agent was much more fulfilling in many ways. My initial enthusiasm over being transferred back to PPD quickly faded as I came to the realization that my main function seemed to be attending a never-ending series of meetings.

As each day passed, I found it increasingly difficult to send CAT teams out on assignments while I remained behind at my desk. Throughout my entire professional life, beginning as a marine officer, I had been a leader, operator, and mission-oriented extremist devoted to accomplishing any task assigned using whatever means necessary while taking care of those entrusted to me. I was now becoming aware of the reality that this type of person, while once valued at the managerial level, no longer seemed to fit into what the Service wanted in its mid- to upper-level supervisors. During the nine years I had spent as an instructor, the Secret Service, along with the entire federal government, had changed dramatically. It was no longer enough for an agent to be merely good at his or her work. In the new Secret Service, anyone aspiring to upper-level management also had to be a diplomat, politically correct, and sensitive to the concerns of various special interest groups that seemed more concerned at times with pushing their agendas than doing their work. I was certainly no diplomat, was totally incapable of political correctness, and had little patience for anything other than accomplishing the mission at hand. In my mind, there remained only two types of agents: those who could do the job and those who could not. To me, all else was nonsense.

One day while sitting in my office staring out the window at the busy streets of Washington as my CAT teams protected the president, the thought of retirement began to creep into the back of my mind. Then, after enduring a particularly painful meeting, the decision to retire began to move from the back of my mind to the front.

The subject of the meeting had to do with making sure the staff of President George W. Bush would not be upset over some of the newer and more obvious and aggressive security measures put in place as a result of 9/11. I remember thinking, *What possible difference could it make what the president's chief of staff or anyone else thinks about how we keep the president alive?*

With President Bush in the Oval Office

(Courtesy of the White House)

I walked out of the office that day carrying inside of me a feeling I had never quite experienced before, something bordering on a strange type of inner peace or tranquility. It was very similar to the feeling I had experienced during my career when death seemed a greater possibility than at other times. Like in Korea at the Bridge of No Return, or in the conference room with the Syrians. When I woke up the following morning, I knew what the feeling was: I was going to retire as soon as practical and felt totally at peace over the decision.

Through the years, I had heard others say that when it is time to retire, an agent just knows. I always wondered if it were true, and on this morning in late April 2004, as the old sages said it would be, I just knew.

I loved the Secret Service, loved being an agent, and had enjoyed a fulfilling career that many at much higher levels had not. I realized, however, that I had become the lion in winter from the Secret Service perspective and simply felt it was time for me to retire while I still enjoyed being an agent and was at the top of my game. After twenty-one years of service, with the winds of social change inside the Secret Service now raging at full force, I realized it was time to move on.

My decision to retire was made easier in that I had just been offered a uniquely challenging position at the Central Intelligence Agency. There was a war on, and I had throughout the years acquired a skill set some at CIA thought would be useful in helping execute their part of that war. At CIA, I would not be behind a desk for the most part, but rather where things were happening. After carefully thinking over their proposition, I accepted this tremendous opportunity to serve in yet another of America's most elite organizations.

Last Night at the White House

My last two weeks in the Secret Service were spent as an acting shift leader on the midnight shift at the White House and on weekends at the presidential retreat at Camp David, Maryland. It was an absolutely perfect way to end my career.

The first time I had entered the White House was fifteen years earlier, as a new CAT agent. Now I was responsible for the safety of the president and his wife, who slept upstairs in the second-floor residence. Should anything, from an attack on the White House to a medical emergency, occur between the hours of 10:00 p.m. and 6:00 a.m., I would be responsible for directing the immediate action of getting the president and First Lady to safety.

On the last night of my operational existence as a Secret Service agent, after things had settled into their usual midnight routine, I walked about the quiet dimness of the mansion thinking about all the years I had spent there. In many ways, the White House felt like home. I thought of the three presidents I had directly protected, my years in CAT, the working shift, running with President Clinton, Christmas parties attended, and driving the president. When the morning came, it was difficult to imagine I was walking out for the last time. I had known it would be difficult.

The Old Ebbitt and Saying Good-Bye

My retirement party was held a few days later at the Old Ebbitt Grill, a bar at 675 Fifteenth Street, a five-minute walk from the White House.

The Old Ebbitt was the place to drink and have dinner in Washington if you were anywhere close to the White House. It was a classy place, where most of the men customers wore suits and the women dressed like women, in skirts and dresses, with pantsuits in short supply—they may have even been against the dress code. It featured a long mahogany bar in the main area, and to the left was a newer addition, where my party was held.

I took a cab there and home because I knew there would be a lot of old friends to see and the night would run late. There were, and it did. There were at least a hundred or so agents in attendance, most of whom had passed in and out of my life and career for the past twenty-one years.

There were many former students there I had helped train. Each seemed to enjoy telling stories of how hard the fitness sessions were and how much they appreciated the severe training they had been subjected to, as well as other lessons learned. With each story told and each drink knocked back, the run distances increased by miles and the heat increased or decreased to levels not able to be endured by humans, until I had trouble recognizing truth from fantasy.

The following day, in a small ceremony at the Old Executive Office Building across the street from the White House, with my wife and son present, I officially retired from the Secret Service. It was May 16, 2004, twenty-one years to the day from when I took the oath of office in Charlotte, North Carolina.

At my retirement ceremony, many of my friends were there from PPD, as well as some young agents from CAT, whom I had supervised and helped train as new agents. My good friend John Mrha was also there and presented each award and plaque due an agent at retirement. The main retirement plaque, which is the Secret Service equivalent of a gold watch, reads in part:

Your twenty-one years of dedication and contributions to the missions and goals of the United States Secret Service are hereby gratefully acknowledged and affirm you to be worthy of trust and confidence.

My family and I left the proceedings and walked to our car outside the White House and then drove home, with the Secret Service behind me and new adventures and challenges awaiting me at CIA. But that is a story perhaps for another time.

Leaving the White House for the last time

(Personal collection of Dan Emmett)

EPILOGUE

B y my retirement in 2004, twenty years had passed since that day in November 1984 when I stood alone in President Kennedy's house contemplating his cuff links. Many great things happened in my life and career during those two decades, including fulfilling my childhood dream of protecting not one but three presidents, as well as the unexpected good fortune of finding the perfect wife. As a result of those great happenings, I am constantly reminded that I was phenomenally lucky to have been a Secret Service agent.

I attained this and other career goals through a determination to succeed hardwired into my DNA at birth and a work ethic instilled by my parents and then welded into place by the Marine Corps. Any disappointments over career goals not accomplished were erased by the many that did come to pass. As a result, I will thankfully never have to look back on my life and wonder what might have been had I only tried to accomplish what some considered seemingly impossible goals.

In addition to having been afforded the honor of protecting the president of our country for almost one-third of my career, I also helped influence a new generation of agents that today drive the Secret Service. That is my legacy to the Service, and in the long run, I consider it to be even more important than the time I spent protecting the president.

Throughout the years I have received e-mails, cards, and phone calls from many former students. The purpose of these communications is to ask how I am doing in retirement, share with me the events of their careers, and many times unnecessarily thank me for my hard but fair approach to training.

The most memorable comments came from a former student named John Hirt. Just months out of the academy, John was shot three times on a routine case by an assailant wielding a 9MM pistol. After suffering the trauma of being shot in the left hip, lower left neck, and back of the neck, with the bullet then entering his right shoulder, John fought with and subdued his attacker. In an e-mail sent to me after the attack, John partially credited his survival that day to the challenging fitness sessions he and his class were subjected to under my tutelage. He wrote that the attitude I helped instill in him and his class of "never give up" was crucial to the outcome of his struggle. John was one of the best students I ever had the privilege of training and is now a great agent and leader in charge of his own office.

John granted me permission to include some of the message in this book, and he writes in part:

"You had a huge impact on all of our lives. To this day, when I talk to any of my classmates reminiscing on our careers, you often come up in the conversation in a positive light regarding those long runs that we could never figure out when they would end. The students you trained will always hold you in the highest regard."

I believe John would have made it through the shooting with or without my training because of the kind of man he is, but I cannot place into words my feelings regarding his comments.

AFTERWORD

Motives for Writing This Work

My decision to write this book did not come overnight, as I retired in 2004 and did not begin this literary adventure until 2010. The final decision to commit my career to paper occurred mainly as the result of frustration brought about by the too many recent books available about the Secret Service that have in some cases not portrayed the organization in an accurate, fair, and objective manner. My primary intent in authoring this work was to present an alternative to some of these other publications by offering an accurate account of what it was like to be a working-level Secret Service agent for over two decades.

Specifically, some of the more current works now available on the Secret Service have been unnecessarily and unfairly demeaning to the organization and have portrayed Secret Service agents as being incapable of discretion, which is not the case. Most agents are fiercely protective when it comes to their jobs and go to great lengths to ensure the privacy of those they protect.

Other books written about the Secret Service have contained stories that are totally false, thereby nullifying any of their relevant moments. For example, I can report with total certainty that, contrary to the assertions contained in one recent book, Bill Clinton never left the White House without the knowledge of the Secret Service. Writings such as I describe have been both damaging and dangerous.

In terms of damage, they can mar and sometimes ruin the relationship of trust that must exist between agent and the president. A president must feel confident that anything confidential or sensitive about himself and his family witnessed or heard by an agent will be kept secret even after the death of that president. Recent publications have no doubt given concern to modern-day presidents over this issue.

As far as danger, materials now available in bookstores and online about the Secret Service sometimes contains far too detailed information about the operational aspects of presidential protection. A writer who publishes any piece containing "Secret Service" in the text, whether in a newspaper, book, or magazine, should be aware that our adversaries will read their work, and the information will possibly be used against us if too revealing.

What is not included then in this book are incidents and episodes I witnessed regarding the private lives of presidents or sensitive information that could provide useful to potential assassins. I could have easily filled volumes with such stories, but to do so would have only contributed further to the already too plentiful, irresponsible journalism available about the Secret Service.

Rather than another tell-all book, I have written about the experiences of a Secret Service agent who protected three presidents of the United States in almost every corner of the world and the events that led to this career. I considered this to be far more important to the written account of the Secret Service than whether Hillary threw a lamp at Bill, as described in a recent book.

ABOUT THE AUTHOR

From May 1983 until retirement in May 2004, Dan Emmett was a Special Agent in the United States Secret Service.

During those twenty-one years, some of his more high-profile assignments included the Presidential Protective Division (PPD) and the Counter Assault Team (CAT), where he provided direct protection worldwide for Presidents George Herbert Walker Bush, William Jefferson Clinton, and George W. Bush. Mr. Emmett's final assignment in the Secret Service was as assistant to the special agent in charge of the Presidential Protective Division.

The author, a former captain in the United States Marine Corps, holds a BS degree in criminal justice from North Georgia College and a master of science in education from Troy University.

Now residing in the southeastern United States with his family, he is an adjunct professor for two universities, as well as a security consultant to both private corporations and the United States government.

APPENDIX 1

Myths and Truths about the Secret Service

Of all federal law enforcement agencies, the Secret Service is perhaps the least understood, due to the multitude of myths attributed to it. Also, there is a culture that exists within the Secret Service totally unique among law enforcement agencies anywhere in the world, and it is as enigmatic as the myths themselves. I have listed some of the more prevalent myths below, followed by their reality and some of the more prevalent cultural aspects of the Secret Service.

Myth: All Secret Service agents protect the president.

Fact: In reality, the vast majority of agents in the Secret Service never directly protect the president, although each by training is qualified to do so. The largest numbers of agents are collectively assigned to other important permanent protection duties, such as the vice president and former presidents.

However, almost all agents when asked if they have protected the president will answer yes. Technically they are correct, although there is an enormous area of subjectivity here. By stating they have protected the president, agents convey the impression that they have served on the Presidential Protective Division when they may not have done so.

For example, all agents throughout their careers are tasked with a function known as "standing post." Standing post is the important function

197

of manning the security perimeters at a presidential event. These agents are not assigned to PPD, but rather to other permanent assignments, such as field offices. By working a presidential event "standing post," they have technically provided protection for that president even though they may not have laid eyes on him. It is then possible for an agent to serve thirty years in the Secret Service having never been assigned to the Presidential Protective Division, while he can accurately state he has protected up to five or six presidents.

As a junior agent assigned to the Charlotte and New York field offices, I stood post hundreds of hours for Ronald Reagan at countless events, but was not on PPD during his presidency. I therefore do not claim having protected him on my résumé, but only George Herbert Walker Bush, William Jefferson Clinton, and George W. Bush, all of whom I protected on a daily basis while assigned permanently to PPD. For most of us who served on PPD, protecting the president means being permanently assigned to that president within arm's length, while those who did not, view the term in a much broader sense.

Another area that lends even greater confusion in this area is the former president scenario. Agents assigned to a former president will usually refer to being on "the detail" and refer to their protectee's status as president in the present tense rather than the past. An agent that was assigned to former President Clinton, for example, will say he was on President Clinton's detail. That agent is totally correct in his statement, but he did not serve on President Clinton's detail while he was a sitting president. It is a game of semantics. If a person truly wants to know the extent of an agent's protective experience, one has to drill down a bit more than merely asking if the agent has ever protected the president. The best question to ask in such cases would be if an agent has flown on Air Force One. If the agent indicates never having done so, the agent was never on PPD.

Only a small percentage of agents will ever serve on the Presidential Protective Division (PPD), and most are hand-selected after years of having proven themselves as field agents or on other protective assignments. Even then, it is not a career-long assignment. Agents that do go to the Presidential Protective Division spend only about five years there, with the balance of an agent's career devoted to other assignments, such as field offices working on criminal investigations or behind a desk at headquarters.

Myth: Secret Service agents are political allies of the president.

Fact: Secret Service agents who serve on the Presidential Protective Division are totally apolitical when it comes to their work. While each has his or her own political views, those views do not influence the level of protection they provide to the president. I have provided direct protection to three presidents, one of whom I did not vote for. I protected that president with the same degree of dedication as I did the other two. This is the norm for all agents.

Myth: Secret Service agents work for the president.

Fact: Secret Service agents work for the director of the Secret Service and the secretary of the Department of Homeland Security. While assigned to the Presidential Protective Division, I was asked countless times how my boss was doing, meaning the president. I would remind all, especially military officers, that POTUS was the commander in chief of the armed forces but not the boss of the Secret Service.

Myth: Secret Service agents swear an oath to die for the president.

Fact: The only oath Secret Service agents take is the oath of office to become an agent. The willingness to possibly get oneself killed protecting the president is never spoken of, but it is nonetheless understood, with no oath or affirmation required.

Big Myth: Being a Secret Service agent on PPD is glamorous.

Fact: For an agent assigned to the Presidential Protective Division (PPD), protection is brutal shift work, with few days off, sleep deprivation, long periods without food or water, and standing for hours in one place. Burnout can begin to occur at about the four-year mark or sometimes even earlier.

An agent works two weeks on day shift, two weeks on midnight shift, two weeks on the evening shift, and then goes into a two-week training phase. At the end of these two weeks, the cycle starts all over again. The changing of shifts every two weeks, combined with constant travel, totally wrecks the body's ability to be on any type of schedule. Ulcers and high blood pressure of agents on PPD are not uncommon. The totality of this lifestyle can also wreck families and marriages, which leads me to the next myth.

Myth: All women are attracted to Secret Service agents.

Fact: Many women are attracted to Secret Service agents. In truth, though, constant separations due to traveling with the president can contribute to failed marriages at a higher rate than most professions. For PPD agents, there is the never-ending string of temptations sometimes literally thrust into one's face by women who are impressed by such things as men who protect the president. It can be almost frightening at times when seated in a bar, and a woman recognizes an agent she has just seen on television with the president. On more than one occasion, my shift mates and I had phone numbers and hotel room keys shoved into our hands or thrown to us while working a rope line with the president. One particularly photogenic agent even received fan mail.

This attention lavished on PPD agents came usually from both young and not-so-young, attractive women intoxicated with the excitement of being so close to the president and those who protected him. It was wild beyond belief at times, and we enjoyed an almost celebrity-like status from the moment we walked down the steps of Air Force One with POTUS until "wheels up." For the single agent, it was paradise; for many married agents, it was a constant struggle between good and evil, which was sometimes won and other times lost.

Female agents on PPD can also attract this type of attention, and I have seen our more attractive agents practically stalked by men seeking strong but feminine women who protect the president and carry guns.

These times of brief celebrity status were just that, however—brief—and do not substantiate the myth of the job being glamorous. It is not.

Myth: Secret Service agents take care of presidential pets.

Fact: All presidential pets, from FDR's Scottie, Fala, to the current White House pets, are walked and taken care of by White House custodial personnel. An agent will make the ultimate sacrifice for POTUS without hesitation, but walking the dog or cat is not and will never be a part of an agent's job description.

A Secret Service agent holding Clinton presidential pet Socks the Cat, with Socks's handler holding the leash. Note Socks's extended claws, indicating he is not enjoying the photo op.

(Courtesy of the White House)

The Unique Culture of the Secret Service

The Secret Service has a culture that is unique in the world of law enforcement. While it shares some similarities in this culture with other agencies, none has quite the same way of doing things as the Secret Service.

The Moving Van

The Secret Service culture is one of an agent selling houses, buying houses, packing, and constantly relocating to a new state, city, or country.

One of the most stressful and difficult aspects of being a Secret Service agent is not the threat of a violent death in the line of duty, but the incessant moving, which inevitably comes on the average of four to six times in a career. Moving, coupled with the constant threat of moving, perpetually looms over most agents. While this is not of great concern for young single agents, it can be a nightmare for older agents with families. This hard and sometimes seemingly unfeeling part of the Service culture surfaces, at times, by necessity, and other times can be purposely inflicted with total indifference by those directing the move.

Any agent can be transferred anywhere at any time based on the ambiguous and subjective policy known as "needs of the Service." Such decisions are ultimately made by headquarters management, who in many cases have moved very little in their own careers and sometimes see agents as mere pins on the map to be moved at will, rather than human beings with families. In all fairness to the Service, however, many transfers also come as the result of an agent's request. During my own career, two of my four moves were by my own wishes, while two were due to the "needs of the Service."

The reasoning used by Secret Service headquarters for subjecting agents to these frequent and sometimes unnecessary moves can be as ambiguous as "the agent has been in one place too long," although no one ever seemed to know how long that was since no such policy exists in writing. Much of Secret Service policy does not exist in writing, but operates on precedence alone.

The other side of this seemingly cold, unfeeling culture will see the Service do anything within its power to help an agent if the physical or mental health of a child is involved. Agents have been allowed to remain in one city for as long as necessary to ensure their child received the best care possible for a condition, and the Service will not move the agent if it could be detrimental to the child. If it is in the best interest of the child's health and welfare to remain in one area indefinitely, then the agent is taken off of the list of possible transferees but will also not be considered for promotion.

I Don't Know When I Will Be Home

The culture of the Secret Service is one of separations due to both the protective and investigative mission. In the history of the Service, hundreds of thousands of children's birthdays, graduations, recitals, ball games, and everything else in between have been missed by agent parents. Many agents are forced to miss these important events due to the nature of the business, but some miss them by choice, engaging in busywork. This is the practice of staying late at the office to do work that could be done during regular work hours. This practice had become epidemic by my retirement, and I was probably not viewed favorably in my open criticism of those who unnecessarily chose work over family in order to score points with management.

Have Some Balls, Agent.

The indispensable trait of courage is also a large part of the Secret Service culture and has been demonstrated by its agents countless times over the years. Many of these examples of courage are well documented, such as Tim McCarthy taking a bullet meant for President Reagan, while many others that occur each day will never be known by anyone outside the Secret Service.

Agents need high levels of both moral and physical courage to face the numerous challenges and dangers inherent over the course of a career. The necessity for this trait in an agent was perhaps summed up best one day at a Secret Service agent graduation in very black-and-white terms.

There is a long-standing tradition at Secret Service agent graduations to invite a keynote speaker. Usually the speaker is a retired agent, due to the fact that many still live in the DC area, thus making them easily accessible. The speeches are usually too long, too hard to follow, too much about the accomplishments of the speaker, and boring. The students, soon to be real agents, have been in training for six months and care little for the keynote speaker's words. They really just want to go home for some well-earned R&R.

While an instructor, I attended many such graduations. One I will never forget, nor will anyone else who attended. On this day, the guest speaker was Red Auerbach, now deceased, former coaching great of the Boston Celtics.

As we instructors sat in our seats looking forward to hearing this icon of American sports speak, we could not help but notice the aromatic scent of a cigar somewhere in the area. Of course, this was not possible, as there was no smoking allowed any longer in government buildings. To light any tobacco product in a government facility could result in death by lecture from some offended, by-the-book type who could recite the regulation forbidding such conduct.

When Red took the podium, it became clear where the aroma was coming from. Red stood there halfway slumping over the podium and microphone, ready to begin his remarks with a lit cigar.

Red began his speech with some amusing anecdotes about coaching the Celtics and kept his audience highly entertained. As he began to wind down, he suddenly became dead serious, paused for effect, stared at the new agent class, and proclaimed in a low bulldog voice to all the newly commissioned agents that throughout their careers they should above all else, "have some balls." (For those of you who are not familiar with the term, it is a metaphor for having physical and moral courage—the willingness to face danger and stand for what one believes, no matter the price.)

As I listened, I thought no truer words were ever spoken. As Red gave this, the most memorable speech I ever heard at an agent graduation, he smoked that giant, wonderfully offensive cigar, with the blue smoke drifting up past the no-smoking signs in the auditorium. Red cared nothing about offending anyone or about some sign proclaiming "no smoking." He had been the invited guest speaker and was going to do and say what he damn well pleased. Red Auerbach came from a time in American history when men drank whiskey and beer with their giant hamburgers and steaks, not daiquiris and white wine with their salads. They also smoked cigars in public places if they wished.

One could almost hear the neopolitically correct upper management from the headquarters eighth floor squirming in their seats on the stage. Many feared with so many civilians in attendance, the Service image would suffer for Red's words. As far as I know, no one complained, and Red Auerbach's words were a good reminder to all in attendance to get back to the basics. To Red, balls mattered, and all should have them, especially in a profession such as the Secret Service. Have some balls; damned good advice, Coach. By the way, no one had the balls to tell or ask Red to put out the cigar.

APPENDIX 2

A Brief History of the Secret Service

W hile most do not discern the difference and constantly interchange the Secret Service with almost every federal law enforcement and intelligence agency in America, the Secret Service is not the Federal Bureau of Investigation or the Central Intelligence Agency. Too many times to count, I have mentioned to someone at a social function or other venues that I worked for the Secret Service, only to have them introduce me to someone else as an FBI agent or a CIA agent.

The Federal Bureau of Investigation (FBI) is the largest federal law enforcement agency in the United States and falls under the Department of Justice, tracing its modern history to the appointment of J. Edgar Hoover as director in 1924. The FBI has a very broad scope of investigative activities, far wider than that of the Secret Service, but the FBI has nothing to do with presidential protection and is in no way officially associated with the Secret Service.

The Central Intelligence Agency (CIA) is the premier intelligence service of the United States but has no arrest authority or law enforcement function. Its primary duty is to gather intelligence in foreign countries and present that intelligence to the president so that he can make better-informed decisions regarding foreign policy. Like the FBI, it too has no direct association with the Secret Service in terms of mission.

The Secret Service is an independent law enforcement agency with full arrest powers, which from its beginning in 1865 until 2002 fell under the Department of the Treasury. After the attacks on 9/11 and a reorganization of American law enforcement, the Service was placed under the Department of Homeland Security, where it remains; it is unique among federal agencies in its dual mission of investigations and protection. The majority of people only think of the Secret Service as the agency that protects the president of the United States. While this is certainly true, the Secret Service is also an investigative agency that helps protect the financial infrastructure of the United States.

Today all US paper currency is printed at the Bureau of Engraving and Printing in Washington, DC. At the conclusion of the Civil War in 1865, however, individual banks produced the country's paper currency, and much of the paper currency in circulation was counterfeit. It was determined that the creation of a federal agency to fight this plague was needed, and this agency would be the United States Secret Service.

Ironically, on April 14, 1865, the day he was assassinated, President Abraham Lincoln signed the bill that brought the Secret Service into existence, thereby creating the agency that would one day protect the president. Even if the Service had already existed, however, it would have done President Lincoln no good. The Service did not begin protecting presidents until thirty-seven years later, in 1901 after President McKinley was assassinated in Buffalo, New York.

The Secret Service was thus originally created for the purpose of combating counterfeiting. This mission of counterfeit suppression remains one of the Secret Service's main investigative missions today and is carried out by field offices that cover all fifty states and most of the world.

In addition to counterfeit investigations, the Secret Service also has the main federal jurisdiction over the statutes regarding credit card fraud and various types of financial crimes, as well as government check forgery. The Service also investigates threats against anyone it provides protection for, most notably the president of the United States.

When a person is hired as a new special agent in the Secret Service, he or she begins his or her career in a field office, which could be located anywhere in the United States, investigating the above-mentioned violations, not on a permanent protective detail. While these investigations have little media appeal, they are extremely dangerous, and one can end up dead while participating in them when least expected—an occurrence that has sadly happened on several occasions.

After an agent serves approximately six years in a field office conducting investigations, he or she may then move on to a full-time protective assignment, such as the presidential detail. This time in the field is really an agent's tryout for protection. If an agent does not prove himself or herself trustworthy, intelligent, proficient with weapons, and hardworking, it is unlikely he or she will ever see the Presidential Protective Division.

In terms of protecting our nation's leaders, which the Secret Service is best known for, it is mandated by law to not only protect the president of the United States and his immediate family, but also the vice president and his immediate family, the president-elect and vice president elect and their immediate families, former presidents and their spouses as well as children under age twelve, major presidential candidates, visiting foreign heads of state if they are in the United States on an official state visit, and anyone else the president so dictates. The Secret Service does not protect members of Congress or the Senate, as is widely believed. That task is performed by the United States Capitol Police.

Only the president and vice president must accept Secret Service protection. All others mentioned may decline protection if they so desire, and many do, most notably numerous foreign heads of state who do not want Secret Service agents around them. The reasons for their refusal of protection range from many believing Secret Service agents to be intelligence officers who will spy on them to preferring that only their own service provide their protection.

As far as Americans entitled to Secret Service protection, only former President Richard Nixon refused. In 1985, eleven years after leaving office and feeling he no longer needed the Secret Service, he hired his own private security, saving taxpayers millions of dollars.

APPENDIX 3

Glossary of Terms and Acronyms

ASAIC: Assistant Special Agent in Charge
ATSAIC: Assistant to the Special Agent in Charge
CAT: Counter Assault Team
CP: Command Post
DSAIC: Deputy Special Agent in Charge
FLETC: Federal Law Enforcement Training Center
Hawkeye: Call sign for CAT
Halfback: Follow-up vehicle
JJRTC: James J. Rowley Training Center
Limo: Limousine
NYFO: New York Field Office
OP: Observation Post
POTUS: President of the United States
PPD: Presidential Protective Division
SAIC: Special Agent in Charge
SAITC: Special Agent Introductory Training Course
SATC: Special Agent Training Course
Stage Coach: Presidential limousine
VPOTUS: Vice President of the United States
VPPD: Vice Presidential Protective Division
WTC: World Trade Center

CPSIA information can be obtained at www.ICGtesting.com
Printed in the USA
LVOW061434300512

283946LV00002B/39/P